CAMBRIDGE
UNIVERSITY PRESS

Cambridge Lower Secondary
Global Perspectives

TEACHER'S BOOK 7

Keely Laycock

CAMBRIDGE
UNIVERSITY PRESS

University Printing House, Cambridge CB2 8BS, United Kingdom

One Liberty Plaza, 20th Floor, New York, NY 10006, USA

477 Williamstown Road, Port Melbourne, VIC 3207, Australia

314–321, 3rd Floor, Plot 3, Splendor Forum, Jasola District Centre, New Delhi – 110025, India

103 Penang Road, #05-06/07, Visioncrest Commercial, Singapore 238467

Cambridge University Press is part of the University of Cambridge.

It furthers the University's mission by disseminating knowledge in the pursuit of education, learning and research at the highest international levels of excellence.

www.cambridge.org
Information on this title: www.cambridge.org/9781108790529

First published 2020

20 19 18 17 16 15 14 13 12 11 10 9 8 7

Printed in Great Britain by CPI Group (UK) Ltd, Croydon CR0 4YY

A catalogue record for this publication is available from the British Library

ISBN 978-1-108-79052-9 Paperback

Additional resources for this publication are available through Cambridge GO. Visit cambridge.org/go

Cover image Gina Pricope/Getty Images, inside image Ishii Koji/Getty Images

Contents

Introduction	v
How to use this book	vi
Approaches to teaching and learning	viii
Active learning	viii
Assessment for learning	ix
Improving learning though questioning	x
Differentiation	xii
Language awareness	xiv
Metacognition	xv
Skills for Life	xvi
Section 1 Research	
Introduction	1
Research skills overview	1
Starting with research skills: Lesson 1	3
Starting with research skills: Lesson 2	5
Starting with research skills: Lesson 3	8
Developing research skills: Lesson 4	11
Developing research skills: Lesson 5	13
Developing research skills: Lesson 6	15
Getting better at research skills: Lesson 7	17
Getting better at research skills: Lesson 8	19
Getting better at research skills: Lesson 9	21
Section 2 Analysis	
Introduction	24
Analysis skills overview	24
Starting with analysis skills: Lesson 1	26
Starting with analysis skills: Lesson 2	27
Starting with analysis skills: Lesson 3	29
Developing analysis skills: Lesson 4	32
Developing analysis skills: Lesson 5	33
Developing analysis skills: Lesson 6	36
Getting better at analysis skills: Lesson 7	38
Getting better at analysis skills: Lesson 8	41
Getting better at analysis skills: Lesson 9	43

Section 3 Evaluation

Introduction 46
Evaluation skills overview 46
Getting started with evaluation skills: Lesson 1 48
Getting started with evaluation skills: Lesson 2 50
Getting started with evaluation skills: Lesson 3 52
Developing evaluation skills: Lesson 4 54
Developing evaluation skills: Lesson 5 56
Developing evaluation skills: Lesson 6 58
Getting better at evaluation skills: Lesson 7 60

Section 4 Reflection

Introduction 63
Reflection skills overview 63
Starting with reflection skills: Lesson 1 65
Starting with reflection skills: Lesson 2 67
Starting with reflection skills: Lesson 3 68
Developing reflection skills: Lesson 4 71
Developing reflection skills: Lesson 5 73
Developing reflection skills: Lesson 6 75
Getting better at reflection skills: Lesson 7 77
Getting better at reflection skills: Lesson 8 79
Getting better at reflection skills: Lesson 9 82

Section 5 Collaboration

Introduction 84
Collaboration skills overview 84
Starting with collaboration skills: Lesson 1 86
Starting with collaboration skills: Lesson 2 88
Starting with collaboration skills: Lesson 3 90
Developing collaboration skills: Lesson 4 92
Developing collaboration skills: Lesson 5 94
Developing collaboration skills: Lesson 6 96
Getting better at collaboration skills: Lesson 7 99

Section 6 Communication

Introduction 101
Communication skills overview 101
Starting with communication skills: Lesson 1 103
Starting with communication skills: Lesson 2 105
Starting with communication skills: Lesson 3 107
Developing communication skills: Lesson 4 108
Developing communication skills: Lesson 5 111
Developing communication skills: Lesson 6 113
Getting better at communication skills: Lesson 7 115

> Introduction

Cambridge Lower Secondary Global Perspectives™ is a transformational programme designed to help students develop a range of key skills that will aid them not only in their school and academic life but also in their future career. At the heart of the course is a varied and active learning approach, which inspires students to explore a wide range of issues and different points of view.

This approach is what I have kept in mind whilst writing a learner's skills book and teacher's book for each stage of lower secondary. Stages 7 and 8 are structured around six skills: research, analysis, evaluation, reflection, collaboration and communication. Stage 9 is structured around five skills (collaboration is not assessed at this stage), and a section dedicated to planning, writing and reviewing the Checkpoint assessment.

Each skills section follows the same approach, guiding learners through a 'Starting with', 'Developing' and 'Getting better at' scaffold, building their awareness of their own progress and encouraging them to take charge of their own learning journey. A range of activities and tasks are included, with plenty of opportunities for peer-to-peer and group work, and to encourage students to reflect upon progress, track action and achievements and record their next steps. The self-assessment activities build on each other to give learners a clear visual of how they are progressing, and these will help you to support them in their learning journey whilst maintaining an overview of any gaps in knowledge and understanding. The learner's skills books are write-in resources, so each learner can create and keep a portfolio of their work and track their progression through each skill and each stage.

The first part of this Teacher's Book includes useful guidance around teaching techniques and pedagogical approaches, with information and tips about things like Assessment for Learning, Differentiation and Language for Learning.

The substance of this book is dedicated to support you when teaching Global Perspectives and in using Learner's Skills book 7 within your classroom. Lesson ideas are designed to help you plan for each stage of your lesson, motivate learners and monitor their progress against learning goals. Worked examples are included for each lesson to illustrate how to build and teach a skill through a relevant Global Perspectives topic, using sample material, exemplars and useful weblinks. This selection of real-life and fictional examples is there to help you plan, but is in no way intended to be a 'correct' way of working through the skills – the ideas are intended to be flexible, and I hope they will assist you in generating ideas to apply to the topic you are studying.

By using this scaffolded approach through each skill and each stage, I hope that you will find a solid framework upon which to build, and that it will support you as an effective facilitator of Global Perspectives, helping your learners to enjoy exploring ideas in the classroom that they can then apply to their lives outside of school and into the future.

Keely Laycock

How to use this Teacher's Book

This Teacher's Book contains both general guidance and teaching notes designed to help you to deliver the content in Cambridge Lower Secondary Global Perspectives Stage 7.

There are **teaching notes** for each lesson of the Learner's Skills Book. Each set of teaching notes contains the following features to help you deliver the unit.

At the start of each section there is a **Skills overview**, which summarises the learning objectives within each skill and how these are developed across the lessons within that skill. It also contains ideas for which Challenge topics can be used, and how you may be able to make links with other skills across the curriculum. Key points cover common misconceptions and tips on how to fill learning gaps. The overview also provides language support, highlighting key terminology needed for that section.

Learning objectives	1.1 Construct relevant research questions 1.2 Identify and begin to reference a range of print and multimedia sources and use them to locate relevant information and answer research questions 1.3 Select an appropriate method and conduct research to test predictions and begin to answer a research question 1.4 Select, organise and record relevant information from a range of sources and findings from research, using appropriate methods
Challenge topic ideas	Education for all; Humans and other species; Disease and health; Conflict and peace; Sport and recreation

The **Learning objectives and Learning goals** feature take the objectives from the curriculum framework and the goals from the Learner's Skills Book, to help you communicate to learners what is expected of them.

CAMBRIDGE STAGE 7 RESEARCH LEARNING OBJECTIVES

1.3 Select an appropriate method and conduct research to test predictions and begin to answer a research question

1.4 Select, organise and record relevant information from a range of sources and findings from research, using appropriate methods

LEARNING GOALS

To get better at:

- understanding when to use primary research methods
- selecting which information to use from primary research
- recording information gained from primary research

Each **How will I know if I reach my goals?** heading contains advice on how students can interact with the success criteria laid out in the Learner's Skills Book.

How will I know if I reach my goals?

Good for: Learners to give examples of their learning from the lesson. They can complete the table at any point in the lesson, but they might do it at the end.

Reflecting the activities in Learner's Skills Book, each lesson consists of advice on how to work through the **Prior learning** activity, **Starter activity**, **Main activity**, **Class discussion** and **Peer feedback**. To help you plan, a suggested time is given against each element of the lesson, and a list of **resources you will need** has been included with each lesson.

Resources needed

Learner's Skills Book 7; your own Language Support handout (if appropriate); text and Challenge topic (e.g. Education for all; see Worked Example for the Main activity).

The **prior learning** notes provide advice on where your learners should be in their learning before beginning the activity.

Prior learning (approx. 5 mins)

Good for: Building on previous knowledge, learning and understanding. This might be from Primary Global Perspectives or from other subject areas as this might be your learners' first Lower Secondary Global Perspectives lesson.

The ideas for the **Starter activity** are designed to grab your learners' attention and create interest and engagement. They include advice on what to listen out for, how to diagnose any issues and how to make decisions about what to do next.

Starter activity (approx. 10 mins)

Good for: Identifying good questions and some of the features of a good question.

The **Main activity** ideas give instructions for successful execution of the activity, with differentiation advice, suggestions for feedback and answers where relevant.

Main activity (approx. 20–25 mins)

Good for: Producing questions about a topic.

Activity: Learners produce a mind map of questions about a topic (can be any topic) in order to produce research questions.

In each lesson there is also a **Worked example** for the Starter activity or Main activity, to demonstrate how the activity could work with a relevant Challenge topic. This serves as an example of what success looks like, but you do not have to use the topic given in the example.

Worked Example for the Main activity

Challenge topic: Education for all

Research Question: Should parents be allowed to decide whether to home school their children instead of sending them to school?

At the end of each lesson there are ideas on how to use the **Independent reflection activity**, **Self-assessments** and **Challenge topic review**, depending on which lesson you are in and if your learners are completing these in the lesson or as homework. These are scaffolded throughout each section.

Independent reflection activity; Self-assessment; Challenge topic review (approx. 15–20 mins)

Good for: Encouraging learners to consider their learning in lessons. Encourage learners to reflect on other skills as well as evaluation skills (research, analysis, reflection, communication, collaboration) they have used this lesson, for example, research skills as they selected which websites to use.

Register to access free supporting resources through Cambridge GO – the home for all your Cambridge digital content. Visit cambridge.org/go

Approaches to teaching and learning

Active learning

What is active learning?

Active learning is a pedagogical practice that places student learning at its centre. It focuses on how students learn, not just on what they learn. We, as teachers, need to encourage learners to 'think hard', rather than passively receive information. Active learning encourages learners to take responsibility for their learning and supports them in becoming independent and confident learners in school and beyond.

Research shows us that it is not possible to transmit understanding to learners by simply telling them what they need to know. Instead, we need to make sure that we challenge learners' thinking and support them in building their own understanding. Active learning encourages more complex thought processes, such as evaluating, analysing and synthesising, which foster a greater number of neural connections in the brain. Although some learners may be able to create their own meaning from information received passively, others will not. Active learning enables all learners to build knowledge and understanding in response to the opportunities we provide.

Why adopt an active learning approach?

We can enrich all areas of the curriculum, at all stages, by embedding an active learning approach.

In active learning, we need to think not only about the content but also about the process. It gives learners greater involvement and control over their learning. This encourages all learners to stay focused on their learning, which will often give them greater enthusiasm for their studies. Active learning is intellectually stimulating and taking this approach encourages a level of academic discussion with our learners that we, as teachers, can also enjoy. Healthy discussion means that learners are engaging with us as a partner in their learning.

Learners will be better able to revise for examinations in the sense that revision really is 're-vision' of the ideas that they already understand.

Active learning develops learners' analytical skills, supporting them to be better problem solvers and more effective in their application of knowledge. They will be prepared to deal with challenging and unexpected situations. As a result, learners are more confident in continuing to learn once they have left school and are better equipped for the transition to higher education and the workplace.

What are the challenges of incorporating active learning?

When people start thinking about putting active learning into practice, they often make the mistake of thinking more about the activity they want to design than about the learning. The most important thing is to put the learner and the learning at the centre of our planning. A task can be quite simple but still get the student to think critically and independently. Sometimes a complicated task does not actually help to develop the students' thinking or understanding at all. We need to consider carefully what we want our learners to learn or understand and then shape the task to activate this learning.

Cambridge Lower Secondary Global Perspectives Stage 7 includes many opportunities for active learning such as pair and group work, discussions, working with a variety of texts; written and spoken, and producing a variety of shared outcomes to raise awareness about global issues, like posters, video clips and podcasts.

Assessment for Learning

What is Assessment for Learning?

Assessment for Learning (AfL) is a teaching approach that generates feedback which can be used to improve learners' performance. Learners become more involved in the learning process and, from this, gain confidence in what they are expected to learn and to what standard. We, as teachers, gain insights into a learner's level of understanding of a particular concept or topic, which helps to inform how we support their progression.

We need to understand the meaning and method of giving purposeful feedback to optimise learning. Feedback can be informal, such as oral comments to help learners think through problems, or formal, such as the use of rubrics to help clarify and scaffold learning and assessment objectives.

Why use Assessment for Learning?

By following well-designed approaches to AfL, we can understand better how our learners are learning and use this to plan what we will do next with a class or individual learners (see following diagram).We can help our learners to see what they are aiming for and to understand what they need to do to get there. AfL makes learning visible; it helps learners understand more accurately the nature of the material they are learning and understand themselves as learners. The quality of interactions and feedback between learners and teachers becomes critical to the learning process.

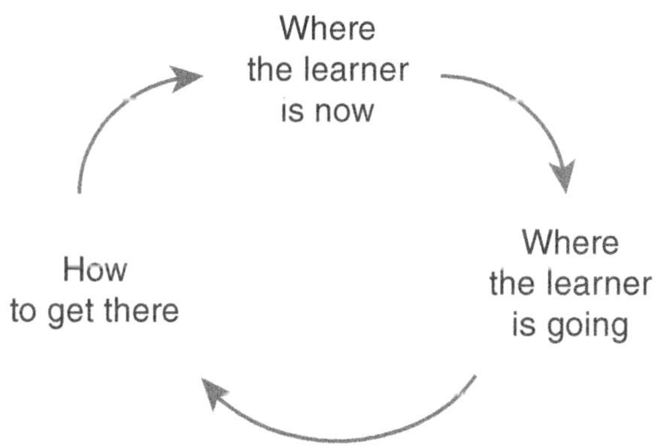

We can use AfL to help our learners focus on specific elements of their learning and to take greater responsibility for how they might move forward. AfL creates a valuable connection between assessment and learning activities, as the clarification of objectives will have a direct impact on how we devise teaching and learning strategies. AfL techniques can support learners in becoming more confident in what they are learning, reflective in how they are learning, more likely to try out new approaches, and more engaged in what they are being asked to learn.

What are the challenges of incorporating Assessment for Learning?

The use of AfL does not mean that we need to test learners more frequently. It would be easy to just increase the amount of summative assessment and use this formatively as a regular method of helping us decide what to do next in our teaching. We can judge how much learning has taken place through ways other than testing, including, above all, communicating with our learners in a variety of ways and getting to know them better as individuals.

Cambridge Lower Secondary Global Perspectives Stage 7 provides teachers and learners with opportunities to check learners' progress against learning goals, give peer feedback and improve work after feedback. For example, improving an argument after peer feedback.

Improving learning though questioning

Thinking is driven not by answers but by questions. Learners do best when they are given adequate opportunities to engage with, and respond to questions. As a teacher, you can use questions effectively in the classroom to:

- review student learning
- challenge learner thinking
- stimulate interest and motivate learners to become actively involved in the lesson
- cultivate critical thinking skills
- encourage learners to ask their own questions.

There are a number of ways in which you can do this.

Depending on the content and aims of the lesson, it is likely that you will use different types of question. Three types of question are explained and exemplified below.

TIP

You should consider the wording of questions in advance to ensure that they are accessible to all learners. This will be particularly important in contexts where the language of instruction is not the dominant language of learners in you class. For help with language awareness, see the document called 'Developing student learners' skills' in this introduction.

Discussion questions

These facilitate debate and allow teachers to dig deeper into learner reasoning (in some situations, their imagination) by asking probing questions.

Example: Why do you think that?

Activity: could be used in pair, small group or whole-class discussion. Discussion questions do not need to have a 'correct answer' as their value is in helping learners to think through, share and discuss their own response.

Diagnostic questions

These give you a quick insight into whether what you have taught has been learned. Responses may identify parts of the curriculum that warrant re-teaching to clarify misconceptions and fill gaps. They can identify specific gaps in learner understanding while learning is still taking place.

Example: True or false?

Activity: could be a lesson starter (using mini-whiteboards or Post-it notes) or part of a quiz or other form of assessment.

All diagnostic questions must have a clear purpose; you must use the information gathered to help inform your next steps. See below for suggestions on how to use diagnostic results in feedback.

Hinge-point questions

The 'hinge' is the point where you move from one key idea/activity/point on to another. Hinge-point questions are a specific type of diagnostic question that are most useful after a period of learning to help you decide whether to continue, recap or re-teach. It is usually the case that understanding the content that occurs before the hinge is a prerequisite for the next chunk of learning. This is important because moving on is dangerous if key concepts are not fully understood, yet if you get this wrong and re-teach pointlessly then engagement will slip and time will be wasted.

Example: What did we learn today? Why does it matter?

Activity: list of ideas (timed), either individually or in a pair. These could be written on poster paper or shared orally.

For hinge-point questions to be useful, you have to be able to elicit the information from learners immediately and be able to understand and act on it quickly. Dylan Wiliam suggests that learners should respond within one minute and teachers should be able to view and interpret responses within 15 seconds. Hinge-point questions seek a response in the form of a snapshot, not an essay.

Experienced teachers will use a range of question types in their professional practice, appropriate to the level, subject and learners they are teaching.

Using feedback to optimise teaching and learning

Questions help learners to challenge and explore their understanding of a particular topic. Questions can also help learners identify areas where their knowledge is less secure. This is a valuable part of the learning process. You can help them to move beyond 'struggle zones' in their learning by providing feedback which helps them to fill the gaps in their knowledge, thereby boosting both their competence and their confidence.

Feedback should:

- be oral or written
- be appropriate to the learner
- include information about where to go (which pages in the learner's book, for example) to revise the problematic material.

Once it is clear to learners what must be done to move beyond their current limits of learning, young people often make significant progress. You can facilitate this progress via feedback and help 'close the loop' of learning.

Feedback is powerful: to optimise teaching and learning, you should create an environment in which learners are encouraged to reflect on their learning experiences and identify next steps during the learning process. These next steps may take the form of further questions on the topic, to which the learners might like to research answers, or the next steps may be connected with their experiences of learning (for more information about metacognition, see the document in this introduction).

Self/peer assessment

Rather than always relying on teacher judgement, by assessing their own (and each other's) work, learners independently assess progress with confidence. Learners who can look at their work, and judge the degree by which it reflects explicitly stated goals or criteria, can assess the quality of their work and revise it accordingly. They are actively involved in the learning process and their independence and motivation is improved.

Further reading

Gaunt, A. and Stott, A. (2019) *Transform teaching and learning through talk: the oracy imperative*, Rowman and Littlefield Education, Lanham, MD.

Gershon, M. (2013) *How to use questioning in the classroom: the complete guide*, Amazon Media.

Paul, R.W. and Elder, L. (2000), *Critical thinking: basic theory and instructional structures handbook*, Foundation for Critical Thinking, Tomales, CA.

Wiliam, D. (2011), *Embedded Formative Assessment*, Solution Tree Press, Bloomington, IN.

Cambridge Lower Secondary Global Perspectives Stage 7 develops learners' ability to not only ask questions like 'what, 'when', 'where' and 'who', but also questions which require more thinking about like 'how' and 'why'. For example, 'How does the amount of water an individual uses impact the issue of global water shortage?

Differentiation

What is differentiation?

Differentiation is usually presented as a teaching practice where teachers think of learners as individuals and learning as a personalised process. Although precise definitions can vary, typically the core aim of differentiation is viewed as ensuring that all learners, no matter their ability, interest or context, make progress towards their learning outcomes.

It is about using different approaches and appreciating the differences in learners to help them make progress. Teachers therefore need to be responsive, and willing and able, to adapt their teaching to meet the needs of their learners.

There is no one style teachers should adopt. Teachers do not need to differentiate everything for everyone every day; instead, they should select appropriate moments in the instructional sequence to differentiate. In other words, effective differentiation is part of an experienced teacher's daily lesson plan. It is important that teachers are able to respond to the needs of their learners and use the techniques they deem to be most suitable.

It can be difficult to fit in all the syllabus content and support all learners, keeping them engaged in their learning. This is a challenge for teachers the world over.

Although there is no single formula that creates a differentiated classroom, when differentiation is in place opportunities for innovation and ongoing reflection are created that boost teaching and learning in a way which would not be possible in a 'one size fits all' lesson.

It is clear how much overlap there is between differentiation and Assessment for Learning methodology. Both aim to support all learners to improve their learning, using similar techniques such as questioning, providing feedback and a learner-centred approach. Ongoing assessment in class is fundamental to differentiation; teachers need to see what the learner currently knows or can do, and then work out what the learner needs to know or do next. It is an approach that incorporates a variety of strategies and depends very much on the individual teacher's school and classroom culture to guide practical implementation and outcomes.

Effective differentiation is heavily reliant on teachers being able to respond to each individual and fully understand their needs to best support their next steps. The viability of this will depend on each teacher's specific context, motivation, obstacles to overcome, and training.

Role of the learner

Understanding individual learners is vital for successful differentiation. In order to be effective, figuring out what the individual already knows or can do is a vital step in the process.

Getting to know learners is, however, more than just finding out what they know. It is also about a broader understanding of learner difference. Learners and their learning can be different for a number of reasons: they may have different levels of interest in the topic; they may have differences in their levels of motivation, their ability to remember information, their confidence, the accuracy of their handwriting, their levels of vocabulary acquisition.

Having knowledge of the individual helps teachers to plan for learning rather than teaching, and ensures that they are always supporting progress. In a differentiated classroom, teachers and learners collaborate in learning and learners have ownership and responsibility. Offering choice can encourage ownership of individual work and learning, creating a learning environment in which learners 'have no fear' and apply effort.

Techniques

Learning outcomes

Since differentiation aims to support all learners in working towards particular outcomes, it is important to carefully consider what those outcomes are and maintain focus on the overarching learning intention and success criteria. Teachers can then formatively assess against these and gauge learner needs.

A shared concept of quality between the learner and teacher is vital for learner progress. This includes both clarity of learning outcome and the use of examples of good work. If learners are aware of what good work looks like, they are better able to both self- and peer-assess.

Scaffolding

Scaffolding, a metaphor to describe the process of learning support that enables learners to go beyond what they are initially able to do, can be a key component of successful differentiation.

These suggestions include the modelling of work and tasks, use of listening and writing frames, provision of sentence starters and structure guidelines, scaffolded use of questioning and the encouragement of group and pair work.

Feedback

Feedback is a key tool in helping all learners to make progress in their learning. Good feedback can help move learners towards their learning outcomes, provided learners understand, act upon and learn from it. Feedback should address any misconceptions that are exposed during learner activities.

Group work

Teachers should employ variety in their classrooms, using a mixture of whole-class instruction, one-to-one work, small group work and peer tutoring. Group work is suggested by many as a good way to differentiate as learners working in groups are able to create knowledge with their peers, help each other to learn, use discussion and apportion tasks based on the relative strengths of the group.

A balance needs to be met between the use of group work and teacher instruction. As John Hattie (2008) argues, direct instruction done properly has a greater impact on learning than group work done incorrectly or inappropriately.

Differentiation support in our materials

Our materials will contain frequent opportunities for ongoing assessment in class to help teachers see what the learner currently knows or can do and then work out what the learner needs to know or do next. This will help to identify misconceptions or misunderstandings and guide actions.

Through the course of the activities in the resources, we will support differentiation predominantly in the following ways:

- differentiation by questioning (embedding questioning strategies to inform better next steps)
- differentiation by grouping (using mixed ability groups)
- differentiation by outcomes (multiple modes of learner output or how learners demonstrate/ show their learning)
- differentiation by task (additional worksheets).

There is no single, optimum way to conduct differentiated teaching. However, we can provide a selection of strategies to help teachers to become more confident in their teaching practice.

Cambridge Lower Secondary Global Perspectives Stage 7 supports differentiation in a number of ways. for example, with each skill section divided into getting started with ..., developing... and getting better at... and by offering learners support via their peers, their Skills Book or by using an appropriate Language Support handout.

Language awareness

What is language awareness?

For many learners, English is an additional language. It might be their second or perhaps their third language. Depending on the school context, learners might be learning all or just some of their subjects through English.

For all learners, regardless of whether they are learning through their first language or an additional language, language is a vehicle for learning. It is through language that learners access the learning intentions of the lesson and communicate their ideas. It is our responsibility, as teachers, to ensure that language doesn't present a barrier to learning.

One way to achieve this is to support our colleagues in becoming more language-aware. Language awareness is sensitivity to, and an understanding of, the language demands of our subject and the role these demands play in learning. A language-aware teacher plans strategies and scaffolds the appropriate support to help learners overcome these language demands.

Why is it important for teachers of other subjects to be language-aware?

Many teachers are surprised when they receive a piece of written work that suggests a learner who has no difficulties in everyday communication has had problems understanding the lesson. Issues arise when teachers assume that learners who have attained a high degree of fluency and accuracy in everyday social English therefore have a corresponding level of academic language proficiency. Whether English is a learner's first language or an additional language, learners need time and the appropriate support to become proficient in academic language. This is the language that they are mostly exposed to in school and will be required to reproduce themselves. It will also scaffold their ability to access higher order thinking skills and improve levels of attainment.

What are the challenges of language awareness?

Many teachers of non-language subjects worry that there is no time to factor language support into their lessons, or that language is something they know little about. Some teachers may think that language support is not their role. However, we need to work with these teachers to create inclusive classrooms where all learners can access the curriculum and where barriers to learning are reduced as much as possible. An increased awareness of the language needs of learners aims to reduce any obstacles that learning through an additional language might present.

This doesn't mean that all teachers need to know the names of grammatical structures or need to be able to use the appropriate linguistic labels. What it does mean is that we all need to understand the challenges our learners face, including their language level, and plan some strategies to help them overcome these challenges. These strategies do not need to take a lot of additional time and should eventually become integral to our process of planning, teaching and reflecting on our practice. We may need to support other teachers so that they are clear about the vocabulary and language that is specific to their subject, and how to teach, reinforce and develop it.

Cambridge Lower Secondary Global Perspectives Stage 7 provides a glossary of terms for use by teachers and learners. Each section in this Teacher Book outlines the subject-specific words and phrases for that section and teachers are encouraged to produce their own Language Support handouts for learners as appropriate.

Metacognition

What is metacognition?

Metacognition describes the processes involved when learners plan, monitor, evaluate and make changes to their own learning behaviours. These processes help learners to think about their own learning more explicitly and ensure that they are able to meet a learning goal that they have identified themselves or that we, as teachers, have set.

Metacognitive learners recognise what they find easy or difficult. They understand the demands of a particular learning task and are able to identify different approaches they could use to tackle a problem. Metacognitive learners are also able to make adjustments to their learning as they monitor their progress towards a particular learning goal. The following diagram shows a helpful way to think about the phases involved in metacognition.

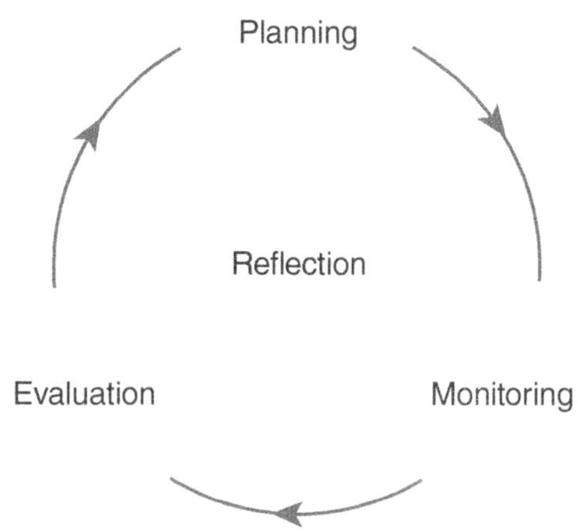

During the planning phase, learners think about the explicit learning goal we have set and what we are asking them to do. As teachers, we need to make clear to learners what success looks like in any given task before they embark on it. Learners build on their prior knowledge, reflect on strategies they have used before and consider how they will approach the new task.

As learners put their plan into action, they are constantly monitoring the progress they are making towards their learning goal. If the strategies they had decided to use are not working, they may decide to try something different.

Once they have completed the task, learners determine how successful the strategy they used was in helping them to achieve their learning goal. During this evaluation phase, learners think about what went well and what didn't go as well to help them decide what they could do differently next time. They may also think about what other types of problems they could solve using the same strategy.

Reflection is a fundamental part of the plan–monitor–evaluate process and there are various ways in which we can support our learners to reflect on their learning process. In order to apply a metacognitive approach, learners need access to a set of strategies that they can use and a classroom environment that encourages them to explore and develop their metacognitive skills.

Why teach metacognitive skills?

Research evidence suggests that the use of metacognitive skills plays an important role in successful learning. Metacognitive practices help learners to monitor their own progress and take control of their learning. Metacognitive learners think about and learn from their mistakes and modify their learning strategies accordingly. Learners who use metacognitive techniques find it improves their academic achievement across subjects, as it helps them transfer what they have learned from one context to another context, or from a previous task to a new task.

What are the challenges of developing learners' metacognitive skills?

For metacognition to be commonplace in the classroom, we need to encourage students to take time to think about and learn from their mistakes. Many learners are afraid to make mistakes, meaning that they are less likely to take risks, explore new ways of thinking or tackle unfamiliar problems. We, as teachers, are instrumental in shaping the culture of learning in a classroom. For metacognitive practices to thrive, learners need to feel confident enough to make mistakes, to discuss their mistakes and ultimately to view them as valuable, and often necessary, learning opportunities.

Cambridge Lower Secondary Global Perspectives Stage 7 encourages learners to develop their metacognitive skills by providing opportunities for individual reflection at the end of each lesson, for example by asking learners to consider what helped them learn best in the lesson and what skills they still need to work on.

Skills for Life

How do we prepare learners to succeed in a fast-changing world? To collaborate with people from around the globe? To create innovation as technology increasingly takes over routine work? To use advanced thinking skills in the face of more complex challenges? To show resilience in the face of constant change? At Cambridge, we have been working on how we can help you with this.

The Cambridge Framework for Life Skills

Many frameworks exist that aim to address the skills and competencies learners' need to succeed through the levels of their education and on into the world of work for the 21st century. At Cambridge, we are responding to educators who have asked for a way to understand how all these different approaches to life skills and competencies relate to their teaching at all levels and support development of the Cambridge Learner Attributes, and how they can support and evidence the development of these skills by their learners through their learning.

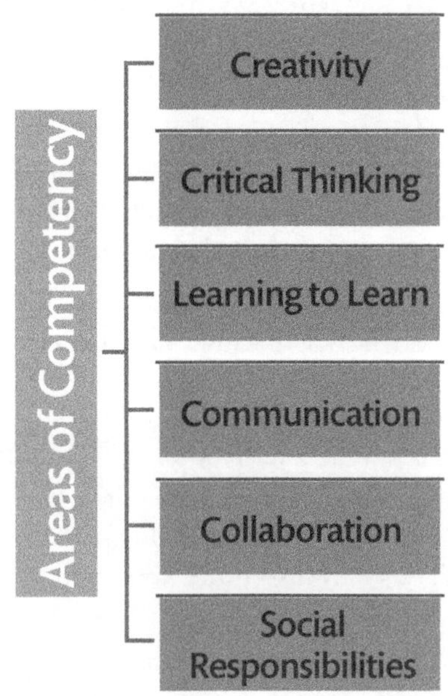

So, we analysed the basic components of these global competencies frameworks and interpreted the different approaches and initiatives to create a common framework of life skills and competencies that can be successfully delivered through teaching at all levels of the Cambridge Pathway.

We have grouped these skills into six main Areas of Competency that can be incorporated into teaching, and have examined the different stages of the learning journey, and how these competencies vary across each stage.

For each of these areas, we have broken down the practical component skills, to help you to understand what each competency involves.

The six key Areas of Competency

The six key skills areas that we will be supporting in our Teacher's Book and Learner's Skills Book are explained below.

1 Creativity

The ability to generate original and innovative ideas or alternatives that are viewed as being valuable and meaningful. Some attributes of creativity are: divergent thinking, imagination, cognitive flexibility, tolerance for ambiguity or unpredictability and intrinsic motivation. We have identified three key competencies within the area of creativity in an educational context:

- the skills needed to participate in creative activities
- creating new content from one's own ideas or other resources
- discovering and expressing one's personal identity and feelings through creative activities.

2 Collaboration

Collaboration is often described as being a key skill for 21st century education. Some advantages of collaboration over individual problem-solving are effective division of labour, use of information from multiple sources, perspectives and experiences, higher level of creativity and quality of solutions. When people are involved in verbal interaction, they are not simply sharing information but they are supporting each other in collective thinking. This collaborative allows participants to achieve more than they can get alone. We have identified three key competencies within the area of collaboration:

- taking personal responsibility for one's own contribution to a group task
- listening respectfully and responding constructively to others' contributions
- managing the sharing of tasks in a project.

3 Communication

Communication is a vital professional and life skill, involving sharing information, ideas and knowledge between people. It is an active process in which elements such as non-verbal behaviour and individual styles of interpreting and ascribing meaning to events have significant influence. Mastering effective communication is a skill learners need for effective and efficient sharing of information, ideas or knowledge in educational and work settings which can be developed and honed at all levels and stages. We have identified seven key competencies within the area of communication:

- using appropriate language/register for context
- managing conversations
- overcoming one's own language gaps
- participating with appropriate confidence and clarity
- supporting others to communicate successfully
- structuring content
- using language for effect.

4 Critical thinking

The higher levels of thinking that learners need to develop enable them to think effectively and rationally about what they want to do and what they believe is the best action. It consists of identifying links between ideas, analysing points of view and evaluating arguments, supporting evidence, reasoning and conclusions. We have identified six key Critical thinking competencies:

- analysing to understand key points and links between ideas.
- evaluating texts, ideas and arguments
- synthesising ideas and information
- identifying and prioritising problems
- evaluating options
- asking effective questions .

5 Learning to learn

It is essential that we continue to learn new skills and knowledge throughout our working lives. The aim of education has to focus as much on the skills of learning as on the outputs of learning. We have identified six key competencies within the area of Learning to learn:

- developing skills for participating in learning
- taking control of one's own learning
- reflecting on and evaluating one's own learning success
- identifying and using effective learning techniques and strategies
- making notes, storing and retrieving information
- managing exam preparation.

6 Social responsibilities

The 'globalised', fast-changing, and multicultural world offers clear opportunities for young people to interact with others and to access information across time and space. However, it also brings challenges of a magnitude no other generation has faced. Climate change, war and conflict, refugees, poverty, gender and social inequality demand global action and a new practice and discourse in the education of young people. Social responsibilities refer to the rights and duties that come along with being a citizen of a particular nation or state, as well as of a broader global entity. We have identified six key competencies within the area of Social responsibilities:

- understanding one's personal and social responsibilities as a global citizen
- behaving consistently with one's personal and social responsibilities
- showing leadership skills
- understanding one's own and others' cultures
- understanding and discussing global issues
- understanding and managing career development options and techniques

Cambridge Lower Secondary Global Perspectives Stage 7 supports all six key areas of competency. Collaboration and communication are the focus of sections 5 and 6 of the Learner's Skills Book. Activities to develop these skills are also contained within other sections of the Learner's Skills Book as are activities to develop creativity, critical thinking, learning to learn and social responsibilities.

Section 1 Research

Introduction

The learning objectives and learning goals for research skills for Stage 7 focus on:

- Constructing research questions
- Developing information skills
- Conducting research
- Recording research findings

However, you might also find opportunities within these lessons to develop some of the other Global Perspectives skills. For example, when recording information, not only will learners be developing research skills, they will also be developing their communication skills.

The ideas given in this Teacher's Book 7 are suggestions only, and the activities can be used with any of the Global Perspectives Challenge topics for Stages 7 to 9, although Worked Examples are provided for some learning activities. It is hoped that the ideas in this Teacher's Book 7 will help you structure your lessons in an active learning way with input from you as the teacher to help guide and support learners to become more effective and independent researchers.

Research skills overview

Learning objectives	1.1 Construct relevant research questions 1.2 Identify and begin to reference a range of print and multimedia sources and use them to locate relevant information and answer research questions 1.3 Select an appropriate method and conduct research to test predictions and begin to answer a research question 1.4 Select, organise and record relevant information from a range of sources and findings from research, using appropriate methods
Challenge topic ideas	Education for all; Humans and other species; Disease and health; Conflict and peace; Sport and recreation
Key points	• Learners think research is about using a search engine, but often don't know how to use a search engine effectively • Learners copy and paste from information sources rather than making notes and writing in own their words • Research does not just have to be from the internet; learners can use books, newspaper and magazine articles, community newsletters, podcasts, videos, interviews with family, friends, teachers and peers, and questionnaires/surveys • Biased and leading questions are questions such as: 'Do you agree that Global Perspectives is interesting?' • Questions that only allow for descriptive responses often start with 'How..?' or 'What...?' For example, 'What animals exist in my country?', 'How do people learn?'

Language support	• Pre-teach key vocabulary: advantages; disadvantages; main idea; subject-specific words; identify; explain; evaluate; home-schooling; evidence; evaluation; judgement; primary research; secondary sources of information; bias; leading question; features; characteristics; data; argument; convincing; reference. Also include any topic-specific vocabulary for the Challenge topics – Education for all; Humans and other species; Disease and health. • Handout of question words with some examples from the topics/subjects: when, what, which, who, where, why and how.
Cross-skills links	2 **Analysis** 2.1 Identify ideas and evidence from different perspectives within different sources on a given topic. 3 **Evaluation** 3.1 Evaluate sources, considering the author and purpose, recognising that some sources may be biased. 3.2 Discuss the effectiveness of a source, making explicit reference to its development of an argument. 4 **Reflection** 4.4 Personal learning: Identify skills learned or improved during an activity and relate to personal strengths and areas for improvement. 5 **Collaboration** 5.2 The team member introduces useful ideas to help achieve a shared outcome and works positively to resolve conflict, solve problems and encourage other team members to participate, when required. 6 **Communication** 6.1 Present information and arguments clearly with some reasoning, referencing sources where appropriate. 6.2 Listen to ideas and information and offer relevant and well-judged contributions that demonstrate understanding of the issue.

Starting with research skills: Lesson 1

Lesson 1 focuses on understanding what the term 'research' means and knowing how to identify and write basic questions.

CAMBRIDGE STAGE 7 RESEARCH LEARNING OBJECTIVES

1.1 Construct relevant research questions

1.2 Identify and begin to reference a range of print and multimedia sources and use them to locate relevant information and answer research questions

LEARNING GOALS

To start to:

- understand what the term 'research' means
- understand how to write some basic questions about a topic
- recognise a good research question
- identify some of the features of a good research question

How will I know if I reach my goals?

Good for: Learners to give examples of their learning from the lesson. They can complete the table at any point in the lesson, but they might do it at the end.

Resources needed

Learner's Skills Book 7; your own Language Support handout (if appropriate); Challenge topic (e.g. 'Education for all'; see Worked Example for the Main activity).

Prior learning (approx. 5 mins)

Good for: Building on previous knowledge, learning and understanding. This might be from Primary Global Perspectives or from other subject areas as this might be your learners' first Lower Secondary Global Perspectives lesson.

Activity: Find out what learners already know about research: What does the term 'research' mean to you?

Differentiation for support: Give learners options:

Research is ... **A** Gaining new knowledge; **B** Using a search engine; **C** Finding out information; **D** Gaining different opinions on a topic.

Suggested answers/ideas: Any reasonable and relevant response. All of the suggestions **A–D** are correct. The intention is to stimulate learners' own ideas.

Not topic specific.

Starter activity (approx. 10 mins)

Good for: Identifying good questions and some of the features of a good question.

Activity: Putting questions into order from best to worst based on some specific features. Explaining what a good research question looks like in a basic way: a question that people care about; a question that is not too broad, too narrow or too vague, a question that allows for information to be found.

Ways of working: Individual, pairs and whole-class discussion on the order of questions and reasons for this order.

Suggested answers: Based on the features, so point learners to these if they are finding this activity a challenge. They should ask themselves: Is the question interesting? Is it too broad? Is it too narrow? Is it too vague? Can it be answered?

Suggested best research question from the choice is question **B** as it is something people care about, not too broad, narrow or vague, and learners will be able to find information to answer the question. **A** is too narrow; **C** is too broad and **D** is too vague and based on a false premise (bad for what?).

Main activity (approx. 20–25 mins)

Good for: Producing questions about a topic.

Activity: Learners produce a mind map of questions about a topic (can be any topic) in order to produce research questions.

Differentiation: Discuss question words already known as starting point: when, what, which, who, where, why and how. Give handout of question word starters or put them on the board.

Ways of working: Individually and in pairs, to share ideas and clarify own thinking.

Whole class discussion based on criteria for a good question (a question that people care about; that is not too broad, too narrow or too vague; that allows for information to be found to answer it). List the best questions from individuals on the board. Encourage learners to identify which question they think is the best question and to give reasons (based on features) why they think this.

Different opinions/perspectives: Also, encourage learners to look at their questions from different perspectives. For example, question 9 in the suggested answers/ questions below will get different responses depending on which perspective it is answered from.

Learner response and feedback: Any suggested questions about the topic should be accepted for the mind map activity. Then encourage learners to focus on the features of a good question to produce their three best questions.

Suggested questions based on the Challenge topic 'Education for all':

1 What is learning?
2 When do we learn?
3 Where can people learn?
4 Where do we learn most?
5 Who helps us to learn?
6 What helps us to learn?
7 What are the benefits of going to school to learn?
8 What are the disadvantages of going to school to learn?
9 Why is learning important (for me, for my community, for my country, for the world)?
10 How do I/we learn best?

Worked Example for the Main activity

Challenge topic: Education for all

Sub-topic: The importance of learning

Suggested best question: Are there more advantages to going to school to learn than disadvantages? It is an interesting question: not too broad, narrow or vague, and can be answered.

Independent reflection activity (approx. 5–10 mins)

Good for: Encouraging learners to consider how they are learning best in lessons. Ask them to be as honest as they can. There is no correct response, and they can choose more than one option. Encourage learners to reflect on other skills (analysis, evaluation, reflection, communication, collaboration) they have used this lesson, as well as research skills. For example, they could say: 'I solved problems with my partner' (the Starter activity), 'I worked in a group sharing ideas for a mind map', 'I thought about and wrote down what helped me learn', and so on. This activity can be done in class, at home or in self-study time.

Starting with research skills: Lesson 2

Lesson 2 focuses on further understanding of the term 'research' and being able to find and record information in the learner's own words.

CAMBRIDGE STAGE 7 RESEARCH LEARNING OBJECTIVES

1.2 Identify and begin to reference a range of print and multimedia sources and use them to locate relevant information and answer research questions

1.3 Select an appropriate method and conduct research to test predictions and begin to answer a research question

1.4 Select, organise and record relevant information from a range of sources and findings from research, using appropriate methods

LEARNING GOALS

To start to:

- understand what research is
- know how to record the main idea from a text
- know how to take notes to help write a text summary

How will I know if I reach my goals?

Good for: Learners to give examples of their learning from the lesson. They can complete the table at any point in the lesson, but they might do it at the end.

Resources needed

Learner's Skills Book 7; your own Language Support handout (if appropriate); Challenge topic (e.g. Education for all) and text for that topic (see the Worked Example for the Main activity).

Prior learning (approx. 5 mins)

Good for: Building on previous knowledge, learning and understanding. This might be from Primary Global Perspectives, from other subject areas, and from their last Global Perspectives lesson.

Activity: Ask learners to remind you what they did last lesson by looking back in their Learner's Skills Book 7. Encourage learners to look at what they thought the best question was in the last lesson and to share with their partner the reasons why they chose this question.

Differentiation for Challenge: Give learners a research question and ask, 'Is this a good research question? Why/Why not?'

Example question from Challenge topic 'Humans and other species': Do humans need animals to survive?

Suggested answers: Remind learners of the features of a good research question from Lesson 1: Is it interesting? Is it too broad? Is it too narrow? Is it too vague? Can it be answered?

Does not need to be topic specific.

Starter activity (approx. 5 mins)

Good for: Identifying where learners might find information.

Activity: Listing where they might find information to answer their research questions.

Ways of working: Individually or whole-class discussion to produce a list on the board and for learners to consider and write down the best way of finding information for the question chosen for the Prior learning activity.

Suggested answers/ideas: Based on the question 'Do humans need animals to survive?': internet websites, specifically organisations such as One Green Planet: http://www.onegreenplanet.org; newspaper articles such as *The Guardian* and *The Huffington Post*, interviews with family and friends, and so on.

Main activity (approx. 25–30 mins)

Good for: Identifying the main idea and subject-specific vocabulary in a text; recording the key information from a text to help write a short text summary.

Activity: Write a sentence on the board twice, such as 'Learning new things can help us try new experiences which might be the best ones we ever have.' In the first of the two sentences cross out all the words apart from 'can', 'us', 'which', 'might', 'have'.

Ask learners:

- Do these words provide information about what the sentence is about?
- Can you guess what the sentence is about, using only these words?

You can make links to English here by asking learners what these types of words are (connector words that don't tell us what the sentence is about and can be used in many sentences, but provide no information about the content of the sentence).

Now cross out all the words from the second version of the sentence leaving 'learning', 'new', 'things', 'help', 'try', new', 'experiences'. Ask learners the same questions as before. This time, you will get a different response from learners. These words are the 'informational' words that give the main information about the content of the sentence.

Tell learners that when they take notes from informative texts, they should only note down the content (subject-specific) words and not the connectors.

1 Give learners a text so that they can identify the main idea and the subject-specific vocabulary. The text should be one from the topic started in Lesson 1; for example, the Challenge topic 'Education for all'. See the Worked Example , 'The benefits of learning at school'.

2 Read through the first paragraph together as a class. Discuss and model note-taking strategies. For example, highlight the informational words only, not the connector words; learners note the key facts and details as single words or short phrases in their own words to show understanding of the information.

3 Learners create a text summary using the sentence starter prompts.

Peer feedback: Learners answer the questions in the Learner's Skills Book 7 to assess understanding of what a summary involves.

Differentiation: Text lengths can vary. Three paragraphs are suggested, but they can be shorter or longer according to learners. You might read the text together as a class, perhaps displaying it on the whiteboard. You can discuss and model reading-comprehension strategies: For example, look at the title, subheadings, illustrations and repeated words for clues about the main idea of the text, find the words that are related to the main idea, and so on.

If learners find producing the summary a challenge, ask them to write a couple of sentences instead of the full summary. They could choose which sentence starters they want to complete, or you can tell them which sentence starters you want them to complete.

Ways of working: Individually, in pairs and whole class to share ideas and clarify their own thinking. Whole-class modelling of working with the text to identify the main idea and subject-specific vocabulary.

Different opinions/perspectives: Encourage learners to see if there are any different perspectives in the text. For example, for the Worked Example, the perspective is very much that going to school is a good idea. This text is written from a personal perspective.

Learner response and feedback: The text summary should be in the learner's own words and should include words/phrases from the tables in tasks 1 and 2. Encourage learners to look back at these two tables to write their text summary.

Encourage peer feedback for the text summary. Summaries should not be too long or short (50–100 words), include the key information and use the learner's own words. Learners should identify one way of making their summary better; e.g. avoid using words/phrases from the text.

Suggested answers: These will vary according to the text.

Worked Example for the Main activity

Challenge topic: Education for all

Sub-topic: The importance of learning

Resource for Lesson 2: Text about the benefits of learning at school

THE BENEFITS OF LEARNING AT SCHOOL

Learning can happen anywhere, but there are many benefits of learning at school.

Here are just three of them:

1 The first benefit is that you have a lot of teachers in one place so can learn many different subjects, such as Maths, Languages and Global Perspectives. Teachers love the subject they teach and spend a long time learning it themselves. They are trained well to teach their subject to different age groups, and they know about the talents of the learners in their class.

2 Another advantage of learning at school is that you are with other people who are the same age as you are. Your classmates might have the same interests which you can do together or they might introduce you to other experiences such as sporting activities like tennis, gymnastics or football. So, as well as learning school subjects, you can also learn how to do other interesting things.

3 Sometimes you have questions about what you are learning and if you go to school there will always be someone there who can answer your questions. You might also be scared of asking a teacher so you can ask a friend in your class to ask instead until you feel more confident.

Suggested answers:

1 a Main idea of text: there are advantages of going to school to learn.

b Subject-specific words: teachers; subjects; trained; talents; classmates; interests; experiences, and so on.

2 The ideas for this response appear in the suggested summary.

3 Suggested summary:

The text is about three reasons why learning is better at school.

The main idea is that it is a good idea to go to school to learn.

In the first paragraph, we find out that we can study many different subjects at school and that teachers are well trained.

The second paragraph is about being with others who might have the same interests as you or who can introduce you to new activities.

The last paragraph tells us that we can ask our classmates if we're afraid of asking the teacher a question and can learn this way too.

Independent reflection activity (approx. 5–10 mins)

Good for: Encouraging learners to consider what they found challenging during the lesson. Ask them to be as honest as they can. There is no correct response, and they can choose more than one option. Encourage explanation but not all learners will be able to do this. Encourage learners to reflect on other skills as well as research skills (analysis, evaluation, reflection, communication, collaboration) they have used this lesson. This activity can be done in class, at home or in self-study time.

Starting with research skills: Lesson 3

Lesson 3 focuses on further understanding of what research is, understanding how to select appropriate research methods and referencing sources of information.

CAMBRIDGE STAGE 7 RESEARCH LEARNING OBJECTIVES

1.2 Identify and begin to reference a range of print and multimedia sources and use them to locate relevant information and answer research questions

1.3 Select an appropriate method and conduct research to test predictions and begin to answer a research question

1.4 Select, organise and record relevant information from a range of sources and findings from research, using appropriate methods

LEARNING GOALS

To start to:

- understand what research is
- know the importance of referencing sources of information
- understand how to choose suitable research methods

How will I know if I reach my goals?

Good for: Learners to give examples of their learning from the lesson. They can complete the table at any point in the lesson, but they might do it at the end.

Resources needed

Learner's Skills Book 7; your own Language Support handout (if appropriate); Challenge topic (e.g. Education for all) and website addresses (see Worked Example for the Main activity).

Prior learning (approx. 5 mins)

Good for: Building on previous knowledge, learning and understanding. This might be from Primary Global Perspectives, from other subject areas, or from previous Global Perspectives lessons.

Activity: Find out what learners found difficult during Lesson 2. Ask learners to write down one area of difficulty and share with the class. Refer learners to the tips in the Learner's Skills Book 7 (Lesson 2) for how they can overcome these difficulties.

Differentiation: Ask specific learners to give the class tips on overcoming any difficulties from the last lesson.

Suggested answers/ideas: Any reasonable and relevant response. Ideas might include:

- to practise with each text at reading through once and then coming up with own headline for the text (main idea)
- to build a list of topic/subject-specific vocabulary for each Challenge (in a notebook)
- to practise reading short texts/paragraphs and writing summaries of no more than 20 words using only own words.

The intention is to stimulate learners' own ideas.

Not topic specific.

Starter activity (approx. 10–15 mins)

Good for: Identifying suitable research methods for specific aims/purposes.

Activity: Group brainstorm and feedback to the whole class. Some learners might find it a challenge to say why they chose the methods they did so this can be used as differentiation for those that can answer at this point. You could come back to this at the end of the lesson.

Suggested answers:

1 Responses will vary

2 I need to find out what local people think and the best way of doing this is to ask some local people.

Discussion:

3 **a** To find out whether I am right about something – internet, books, ask teacher/friend/parent

b To find out what the government of a country thinks about something – internet, government websites, newspaper article

c To find out what my friends and family think about something – questionnaire, interview.

Not topic specific.

Main activity (approx. 20–25 mins)

Good for: Seeing the importance of giving credit to other people's work and not just copying it as your own.

Activity: You might start by having a discussion and asking learners the following questions (Some suggested answers have been put in brackets):

- Do you think anything bad might happen to you if you copy someone else's words or ideas and don't give them any credit? (No or bad grade, kicked out of school, lose people's faith/trust in you as they think you are a cheat, etc.)
- How do you think you might feel if someone stole your words and ideas and didn't give you any credit? What do you think should happen to them if they do? Should they get a bad or no grade?
- Why do you think it might be unfair to use someone else's work without giving them any credit?
- How would you feel if you posted something on social media and your friends shared it as if it were their own post and didn't give you any credit?
- How does it help you if you say where you got your information from? (Shows I know where to look and what I am talking about and that I have understood the information I have read from the source.)
- How does it help someone who reads your work if you say where you got your information from? (They can learn more from the sources of information you have used, they can see that you have used good sources so can trust what you are saying, etc.)
- How do you think you might give credit to other people's words and ideas in your own work? (By citing and by including a reference list at the end of a piece of work.)
- What information do you think you need to give credit for? (Someone else's idea or opinion, any facts, statistics, graphs and drawings, quotations of someone else's spoken or written words, paraphrases of someone else's spoken or written words.)

After class discussion, learners can do the activities in their Learner's Skills Book 7, sharing with a partner why a reference list is important.

Differentiation: For task 3, revisit the work on the main idea, referring learners back to Lesson 2. Give a pair of learners the same website address or addresses; they might work on their own and then share. Or give the whole class a set of website addresses, and for each one they note the main idea and then share. You might make up some website addresses with the main idea in them, e.g. https//whatcanwedo/plastic/use/local.by

You can also use newspaper articles if you have no access to the internet. For each article, learners record the main idea. For task 4, learners can write a reference for each newspaper article. For this, they need to record the author, the title of the article, the date it was published and the title of the news agency that published the article.

Ways of working: Individually and in pairs to share ideas and clarify own thinking. Whole-class discussion based on the importance of referencing and how to reference sources of information.

Different opinions/perspectives: Also, encourage learners to look at the website addresses and think about which perspective they think the ideas on the website come from. For example, for the Worked Example below: 1 Home-schooling/parents/global; 2 Australian government/national; 3 The Gurugram school/India/national; 4 China/national; 5 Technology/global

Learner response and feedback: Stress that, at the moment, it doesn't matter that learners don't do referencing correctly as this is a skill that can be developed over the next levels (Developing … and Getting better at …) and Stages 8 and 9, but they should try to reference other people's work and keep a list of sources of information they use. Peer feedback so learners can clarify their own understanding and gain ideas from their peers – an important part of learning about referencing.

Suggested answers based on the Challenge topic 'Education for all': There are many different systems for citing and referencing sources of information. One in common use internationally is Harvard. To cite in Harvard in the text, the author and date go in brackets after the information within the written work (Wiggins, 2016). The full reference including author, date and title of the article, web address and date accessed go in an author alphabetical reference list at the end of the piece of work. Footnotes are not used in the Harvard system. So the full reference for the citation given is:

Wiggins (2016). *Students Learn Best When You Do This*. Teachthought [online] Available at: https://www.teachthought.com/pedagogy/students-learn-best (Accessed 2/12/2019).

Worked Example for the Main activity

Challenge topic: Education for all

Sub-topic: The importance of learning

The weblinks below are examples of how to reference web addresses correctly – they may not necessarily be active links, as these often change. You can either use these, or find your own and follow the same formatting.

1 https://www.theguardian.com/lifeandstyle/2016/sep/10/10-good-reasons-to-home-school-your-child (main idea – benefits of being educated / learning at home rather than at school)

Full reference: Barbieri (2016). *10 good reasons to home school your child. The Guardian.* [online] Available at: https://www.theguardian.com/lifeandstyle/2016/sep/10/10-good-reasons-to-home-school-your-child (Accessed 21/09/2018).

2 http://raisingchildren.net.au/articles/learning_primary_secondary_school.html (main idea – how children and teenagers learn)

Full reference: Raising Children Network (2016). *Learning: Primary and secondary school years.* Raising Children Network. [online] Available at: https://raisingchildren.net.au/articles/learning_primary_secondary_school.html (Accessed 21/09/2018).

3 https://www.hindustantimes.com/gurugram/the-gurugram-school-that-has-one-class-for-96-students/story-BFPAt9HvBCjvXX9gvAwpSK.html (main idea – No space and crumbling building forces learning in an area with a leaking roof)

Full reference: HT correspondent (2018). *The Gurugram school that has one class for 96 students.* Hindustani Times. [online] Available at: https://www.hindustantimes.com/gurugram/the-gurugram-school-that-has-one-class-for-96-students/story-BFPAt9HvBCjvXX9gvAwpSK.html (Accessed 21/09/2018).

4 https://www.dragonsocial.net/blog/education-in-china (main idea – the problems of education in China)

Full reference: Thai (2017). *Education in China: The Good, The Bad & The Big Opportunities.* Dragon social. [online] Available at: https://www.dragonsocial.net/blog/education-in-china (Accessed 21/09/2018).

5 https://www.theguardian.com/sustainable-business/technology-empower-children-developing-countries (main idea – the use of technology for learning)

Full reference: Kelly (2013). *Technology can empower children in developing countries – if it's done right.* The Guardian. [online] Available at: https://www.theguardian.com/sustainable-business/technology-empower-children-developing-countries (Accessed 21/09/2018).

Independent reflection activity; Self-assessment; Challenge topic review (approx. 15 –20 mins)

Good for: Encouraging learners to consider their learning in lessons. Ask them to be as honest as they can. There is no correct response, and they can choose more than one option. Encourage learners to reflect on other skills as well as research skills (analysis, evaluation, reflection, communication, collaboration) they have used this lesson, for example, collaboration skills as they discussed with a partner.

Learners also complete the self-assessment to set their own learning targets before they move on. Learners think about and shade where they think they are at this time in their learning. 'With help' refers to guidance given (pointing a learner in the right direction, although examples should still come from the learner), for example, from you, other learners or previous work done by the learner in the Learner's Skills Book 7. For the Challenge topic review, learners explore the topic used in this section to develop research skills. These activities can be done in class, at home or in self-study time.

Suggested examples:

1.1 *Construct relevant research questions.* Features of a good research question: a question that people care about; a question that is not too broad, too narrow or too vague; a question that allows for information to be found/an answer. Good research questions: 'Is home-schooling better than learning at school?' 'Do humans need animals for survival?'

1.2 *Identify and begin to reference a range of print and multimedia sources and use them to locate relevant information and answer research questions.* To acknowledge/recognise someone else's ideas; referencing, for example, Wiggins (2016). *Students Learn Best When You Do This.* Teachthought [online] Available at: https://www.teachthought.com/pedagogy/students-learn-best/ (Accessed 2/12/2019).

1.3 *Select an appropriate method and conduct research to test predictions and begin to answer a research question.* Research methods include: Interview, questionnaire/survey, internet search, Look in newspaper, magazine, book. To know what family/friends think, use interview, questionnaire, survey.

1.4 *Select, organise and record relevant information from a range of sources and findings from research, using appropriate methods.* Any relevant example.

Developing research skills: Lesson 4

Lesson 4 focuses on the features of a good research question and how to start constructing research questions. It follows on from work done in Lesson 1 to develop learners' understanding of what a good research question looks like and how to write as well as identify good and bad research questions.

CAMBRIDGE STAGE 7 RESEARCH LEARNING OBJECTIVES

1.1 Construct relevant research questions

LEARNING GOALS

To develop knowledge and understanding about:

- the features of a good research question
- how to write a good research question
- how to write sub-questions to help answer research questions

How will I know if I reach my goals?

Good for: Learners to give examples of their learning from the lesson. They can complete the table at any point in the lesson, but they might do it at the end.

Resources needed

Learner's Skills Book 7; your own Language Support handout (if appropriate); Challenge topic (e.g. 'Education for all – Learning at home instead of at school'); see Worked Example for the Main activity.

Prior learning (approx. 5 mins)

Good for: Building on previous knowledge, learning and understanding. This might be from Primary Global Perspectives, from other subject areas, or from Global Perspectives lessons (especially Lesson 1).

Activity: Review learning from Lesson 1: Features of a research question – a question that people care about, a question that is not too broad, too narrow or too vague, a question that allows for information to be found/an answer.

Differentiation: Allow learners to look back in their Learner's Skills Book 7. Some will not need to. Learners can work in pairs for support.

Suggested answers: Any reasonable and relevant response, but responses will be from Lesson 1.

Not topic specific.

Starter activity (approx. 10 mins)

Good for: Judging the quality of research questions using features already discussed.

Activity: Giving reasons for their judgement of the quality of the research questions.

Ways of working: Individually, in pairs and whole-class discussion.

Suggested answers/ideas:

1 A fairly good question. People care about this topic; it is not too broad, too narrow or too vague, and information can be found. However, you might want learners to consider whether it is arguable (for later in the lesson).

2 Not such a good question. People do care about the issue, but it's a little narrow as it focuses just on Neverland. There is unlikely to be very much information to answer the question.

3 A good question. People care about this issue; it's not too broad, narrow or vague, and there is information about it. It can also be argued.

Main activity (approx. 20–25 min)

Good for: Making research questions even better. Explores further features of a good research question.

Activity: Discussion about all the features of a good research question, including:

- Clear: Does the sentence structure of the question make sense? Is it a question? Would someone else know what you are asking?

- Focused: Is the question too broad, making it hard to answer? Is the question too narrow, making it hard to find enough information?
- Arguable: Does your research question allow you to form an opinion? Does it allow you to support this opinion with evidence?

Differentiation: Learners can work in pairs for support. You could create a handout with all the features of a good research question on it (Is it interesting? Is it too broad, narrow or vague? Can it be answered? Is it clear? Is it focused? Is it arguable?) Handouts can also have explanations and examples on.

Ways of working: Individually and in pairs to share ideas and clarify own thinking. Whole-class discussion about features of a good research question.

Different opinions/perspectives: Encourage learners to see if their questions can be answered from different perspectives: global, local, national.

Learner response and feedback: Encourage learners to give feedback to each other based on the features of a good research question.

Suggested answers based on the Challenge topic 'Education for all':

Learners are developing their ability to write good research questions so any reasonable questions to do with the topic. Stress the importance of using the features when judging the quality of research questions (see Worked Example).

Worked Example for the Main activity

Challenge topic: Education for all

Research Question: Should parents be allowed to decide whether to home school their children instead of sending them to school?

Suggested answers/ideas:

1 I am interested in this topic because I want to find out more about different ways of getting an education.

2 Questions to do with the topic:

   a What are the benefits of home-schooling?

   b What are the disadvantages of home-schooling?

   c Why do parents decide to home school their children?

3 Depends on the questions. In this example, questions **a** and **b** are 'What' questions that lend themselves to a descriptive response and are not arguable, and question c is a 'Why' question that also lends itself to a descriptive response and is not an arguable question. They are all too narrow in focus. For example, just focusing on the benefits or disadvantages of one type of schooling or on one group of people, e.g. parents.

4 One possible research question could be: 'Should parents be allowed to decide whether to home-school their children instead of sending them to school?'

5 The question in task 4 is interesting (from a Global Perspectives viewpoint), is clear, lends itself more to analysis than description, is not too broad or narrow in focus, and is arguable.

7 Learners can discuss their question with their classmates to see if they think it's a good research question or whether it needs rewording.

8 A reworded example might be: 'Is it better to be home-schooled or to learn in a school environment?'

9 Three sub-question examples: 'Who decides whether children have to go to school?'; 'What sort of children benefit from home-schooling?'; 'Do all children benefit from learning at school?'

Independent reflection activity (approx. 5–10 mins)

Good for: Encouraging learners to consider their learning from the lesson. They should apply what they have learned to judge the quality of the question: 'Can sporting events bring about world peace?'

The question is interesting, not too narrow or vague, but might be a little too broad. Perhaps change 'sporting events' to 'The Olympics'. The question is clear and mostly well-focused and it is arguable, so overall, a good question. It can also be answered from a global and national perspective. Encourage learners to reflect on other skills as well as research skills (analysis, evaluation, reflection, communication, collaboration) they have used this lesson. This activity can be done in class, at home or in self-study time.

Developing research skills: Lesson 5

Lesson 5 focuses on the difference between primary and secondary research methods and how to produce a questionnaire to get information from people. It follows on from work done in Lesson 2 to develop learners' understanding of selecting appropriate research methods.

CAMBRIDGE STAGE 7 RESEARCH LEARNING OBJECTIVES

1.3 Select an appropriate method and conduct research to test predictions and begin to answer a research question

LEARNING GOALS

To develop knowledge and understanding about:

- the difference between different research methods
- the characteristics of good and bad research questions
- writing questions for a questionnaire to gain information about an issue

How will I know if I reach my goals?

Good for: Learners to give examples of their learning from the lesson. They can complete the table at any point in the lesson, but they might do it at the end.

Resources needed

Learner's Skills Book 7; your own Language Support handout (if appropriate); Challenge topic (e.g. Disease and Health; see Worked Example for the Main activity) but any topic suitable.

Prior learning (approx. 5–10 mins)

Good for: Building on previous knowledge, learning and understanding. This might be from Primary Global Perspectives, from other subject areas, or from Global Perspectives lessons (especially Lesson 2).

Activity: Review learning from Lesson 2: Selecting the most suitable research methods depending on who you want information from.

Differentiation: Allow learners to look back in their Learner's Skills Book 7. Some will not need to. Learners to work individually and then share ideas with a partner/whole class.

Suggested answers/ideas: Any reasonable and relevant response.

A	Teacher	3	Interview
B	Peers in a different school	1	Questionnaire (or 2 Survey)
C	National government	4	Internet
D	Local people	2	Survey (or 3 Interview)

Reasons will vary. If looking for a national perspective, secondary research methods (internet, books, national newspapers) are more likely to be used. If looking for a more local perspective (school, community), primary research methods (interviews, survey, questionnaire) are more likely to be used.

Not topic specific.

Starter activity (approx. 10 mins)

Good for: Discussion about the characteristics of questions for a questionnaire to conduct primary research.

Activity: Choosing important characteristics of questions for primary research questionnaires. Giving reasons for choice and any changes in choice after discussion.

Ways of working: Individually, in pairs and whole-class discussion.

Suggested answers:

A Important as the researcher needs to be able to use the information gained.

B Important to inform an answer to the research question.

C Important if you want people to answer the questionnaire.

D Important or will lead to confusion and people not answering or answering incorrectly.

E Important as you want to find out what others think not clarify your own thinking. You want to gain authentic responses from people about the issue.

No correct answer.

Not topic specific.

Main activity (approx. 20–25 mins)

Good for: Identifying good and bad questions when writing questionnaires.

Activity: Discussion about why the questions are good/bad relating to clarity, topic and purpose of research and whether the questionnaire contains bias or are leading questions.

Differentiation: Learners can work in pairs for support. You could look back at the Starter activity. Learners can rewrite the questionnaire, rewording some questions, removing questions or adding questions so they still have ten questions. Individual work or in pairs for support.

Ways of working: Individually and in pairs to share ideas and to clarify own thinking. Whole-class discussion about good/bad questions on questionnaires to conduct primary research.

Different opinions/perspectives: Encourage learners to see that questions 2, 4, 6, 9 and 10 are designed to gain their personal perspective (even if some are not very good questions), which might be different to the perspective of their peers.

Learner response and feedback: Encourage learners to discuss in pairs / as a class about the quality of the questions once they've had time to answer the questions.

Suggested answers based on the Challenge topic 'Disease and Health':

Learners are developing their ability to write good questions by evaluating the questions from the Worked Example so any reasonable response is acceptable. Refer them back to the Starter activity and to the tips in the Learner's Skills Book 7.

Questions should:

- be worded so that the researcher gets the information they need
- relate to the topic and purpose of the study
- be able to be answered fairly quickly
- be clear in what they are asking
- not be leading.

See Worked Example .

Worked Example for the Main activity

Challenge topic: Disease and Health

PRIMARY RESEARCH QUESTIONNAIRE: TO FIND OUT ABOUT EATING HABITS

Name: ....

1 How many pieces of fruit and vegetables do you eat in a day?

0–2 ☐ 3–5 ☐ 6–8 ☐ 9 or more ☐

2 Do you agree that apples are better than oranges?

Yes ☐

3 How many burgers do you eat in a week?

None ☐ A lot ☐

4 Do you think fast food is bad for you?

Yes ☐ No ☐

Why? ....

....

5 How often do you do your English homework?

Always ☐ Never ☐

6 Do you or do you not like eating the following foods?

Bread ☐ Pasta ☐ Rice ☐ Beans ☐

7 How much TV do you watch?

None ☐ Up to an hour ☐ 1–2 hours ☐

8 How often do you eat salad?

Never ☐ 1–2 times per week ☐

3–4 times per week ☐

5 or more times per week ☐

9 Do you like chocolate?

Yes ☐

10 Do you agree that smoking is bad for you?

Yes ☐

Thank you for filling in my questionnaire.

Suggested answers:

Name – Probably doesn't need including unless you want to follow up with further questions/an interview.

1 A good question as it is clear, specific and related to the purpose. It could be broken down further

into one question about fruit and another about vegetables.

2 A leading question with only one option so not a good question. It could be improved with the addition of a 'no' option.

3 Related to the purpose but not specific (lacking in choices) and open to interpretation as to what is meant by 'a lot'.

4 A fairly good question because of the space to explain. However, as it might take time people might not answer the 'why' part, and therefore, the answer won't give much information. Bad for what? Also, it depends on what is meant by 'fast food' as healthy food can be 'fast'.

5 Not relevant to the topic or purpose.

6 Not clear enough as two choices in the one question.

7 Not relevant to the topic or purpose.

8 A good question – clear, specific and related to purpose and topic.

9 A leading question as only one option available.

10 A leading question and not relevant to the purpose.

Independent reflection activity (approx. 5–10 mins)

Good for: Encouraging learners to consider how they helped someone else learn today. Encourage learners to reflect on other skills as well as research skills (analysis, evaluation, reflection, communication, collaboration) they have used this lesson. This activity can be done in class, at home or in self-study time.

Developing research skills: Lesson 6

Lesson 6 focuses on designing a questionnaire to gain information to help answer a research question. It follows on from Lesson 5, identifying characteristics of a good question for a questionnaire.

CAMBRIDGE STAGE 7 RESEARCH LEARNING OBJECTIVES

1.3 Select an appropriate method and conduct research to test predictions and begin to answer a research question

1.4 Select, organise and record relevant information from a range of sources and findings from research, using appropriate methods

LEARNING GOALS

To develop knowledge and understanding about:

- how to write a questionnaire to gain information
- recording information gained from primary research

How will I know if I reach my goals?

Good for: Learners to give examples of their learning from the lesson. They can complete the table at any point in the lesson, but they might do it at the end.

Resources needed

Learner's Skills Book 7; your own Language Support handout (if appropriate); a picture of many learners in a classroom (see Worked Example for the Starter activity); Challenge topic (e.g. 'Education for all – Is school the best place for learning to happen?')

Prior learning (approx. 5–10 mins)

Good for: Building on previous knowledge, learning and understanding. This might be from Primary Global Perspectives, from other subject areas, or from previous Global Perspectives lessons (especially Lesson 5).

Activity: Review learning from Lesson 5: Characteristics of a good question for primary research. Emphasise that questions should be worded so that:

- the researcher gets the information they need
- the questions relate to the topic and purpose of the study

- they can be answered fairly quickly
- are clear in what they are asking
- they do not contain bias and are not leading questions.

Differentiation: Allow learners to look back in their Learner's Skills Book 7. Some will not need to. Learners can work in pairs for support. Whole-class discussion to clarify which are good questions and why.

Suggested answers: Any reasonable and relevant response according to the characteristics (above).

A is a leading question with only one choice so it is not a good question.

B is a good question with two choices but also space for other answers. It is clear, related to the topic and not a leading question or biased.

C is a good question with three possible answers, relates to the topic, is clear and not a leading question or biased.

D is clear and relates to the topic but only gives two choices. The question could be improved if it had 'other' as one of the choices for people to complete as in question B.

Starter activity (approx. 10–15 mins)

Good for: Revisiting question words in preparation for writing a questionnaire.

Activity: Asking questions about a picture. Giving reasons for their choice of their partner's best question.

Ways of working: Individually, in pairs and whole-class discussion.

Suggested answers:

Depends on the picture. See Worked Example .

Any reasonable questions can be accepted, there are no correct answers.

Worked Example for the Starter activity

Challenge topic: Education for all

Picture of many learners in a classroom. Any relevant picture depending on the topic used for developing research skills.

Example questions:

When is this lesson?

What are the students learning?

Which of these students doesn't understand the question?

Who is teaching the class?

Where is the lesson being taught?

Why are there so many students in the class?

How does the teacher know who is not learning?

Any reasonable questions can be accepted, there are no correct answers.

Main activity (approx. 20–25 min)

Good for: Creating questions for a primary research questionnaire to gain information related to the topic.

Activity: Give learners the topic and purpose of their study. For example: 'Is school the best place for learning to happen?' Subsequent lessons build on this particular research question. Should you wish learners to do a different topic, note that they will use the same research question in Lessons 6, 7, 8 and 9.

Differentiation: Learners can work in pairs for support. Put characteristics of good questions on the board or refer learners back to the 'Tips' in their Learner's Skills Book 7.

Ways of working: Pairs to share ideas, clarify own thinking and as support. Pairs can share with another pair for questionnaire evaluation in task 2.

Different opinions/perspectives: Encourage learners to write questions to gain different opinions about whether school is the best place for learning.

Learner response and feedback: Encourage learners to give feedback to each other by answering the questions and considering how they might improve their questionnaire.

Suggested answers based on the Challenge topic 'Education for all':

Learners are developing their ability to write good questions to conduct primary research so any reasonable questions to do with the topic. Stress the importance of using the characteristics of good questions for primary research when judging the quality of research questions.

Ask learners to give their questionnaire to ten of their classmates to complete before the next lesson. They should collect in the completed questionnaires and bring them to the lesson.

Independent reflection activity; Self-assessment; Challenge topic review (approx. 15–20 mins)

Good for: Encouraging learners to consider their learning and progression in learning in lessons. Ask them to be as honest as they can. Encourage learners to reflect on other skills as well as research skills (analysis, evaluation, reflection, communication, collaboration) they have used this lesson, for example, evaluation skills as they give feedback on each other's work.

Learners also complete the self-assessment to set their own learning targets before they move on. Learners look back at previous self-assessment and think about and shade where they think they are at this time in their learning. 'With help' refers to guidance given (pointing a learner in the right direction, although examples should still come from the learner), for example, from you, other learners and previous work done by the learner in the Learner's Skills Book 7. For the Challenge topic review, learners explore the topic used in this section to develop research skills. These activities can be done in class, at home or in self-study time.

Suggested examples:

1.1 *Construct relevant research questions.* Features of a good research question: a question that people care about; a question that is not too broad, too narrow or too vague, a question that allows for information to be found/an answer. Good research questions: 'Is home-schooling better than learning at school?', 'Do humans need animals for survival?'

1.2 *Identify and begin to reference a range of print and multimedia sources and use them to locate relevant information and answer research questions.* To acknowledge/recognise someone else's ideas; Wiggins (2016). *Students Learn Best When You Do This*. Teachthought [online] Available at: https://www.teachthought.com/pedagogy/students-learn-best/ (Accessed 2/12/2019).

1.3 *Select an appropriate method and conduct research to test predictions and begin to answer a research question.* Primary research is important to get first-hand accounts of events or to gain opinions/viewpoints from different people. Primary research methods include interviews, surveys, questionnaires and blogs. Secondary research methods include textbooks, internet articles, newspaper and magazine articles, and biographies.

1.4 *Select, organise and record relevant information from a range of sources and findings from research, using appropriate methods.* Any relevant example. Can use examples from their Learner's Skills Book 7 from Lesson 5.

Getting better at research skills: Lesson 7

Lesson 7 focuses on the use of primary research to gain information and how to organise and record the information gained from primary research. It follows on from work done in Lessons 5 and 6.

CAMBRIDGE STAGE 7 RESEARCH LEARNING OBJECTIVES

1.3 Select an appropriate method and conduct research to test predictions and begin to answer a research question

1.4 Select, organise and record relevant information from a range of sources and findings from research, using appropriate methods

LEARNING GOALS

To get better at:

- understanding when to use primary research methods
- selecting which information to use from primary research
- recording information gained from primary research

How will I know if I reach my goals?

Good for: Learners to give examples of their learning from the lesson. They can complete the table at any point in the lesson, but they might do it at the end.

Resources needed

Learner's Skills Book 7; your own Language Support handout (if appropriate); text (see the Worked Example for the Starter activity); Challenge topic (e.g. 'Education for all' to help answer the research question: 'Is school the best place for learning to happen?' from Lesson 6, or any other topic learners wrote their questionnaire about in Lesson 6).

Prior learning (approx. 5–10 mins)

Good for: Building on previous knowledge, learning and understanding. This might be from Primary Global Perspectives, from other subject areas, or from previous Global Perspectives lessons (especially Lessons 5 and 6).

Activity: Review learning about primary research and its purpose from Lesson 6.

Differentiation: Allow learners to look back in their Learner's Skills Book 7. Some will not need to. Learners to work individually and then share ideas with a partner/whole class.

Suggested answers: Any reasonable and relevant response.

Primary research helps us:

- understand experiences and events from people who were actually there (first-hand)
- gain viewpoints and opinions about different things from different groups of people
- answer research questions from a particular viewpoint/perspective.

Not topic specific.

Starter activity (approx. 10–15 mins)

Good for: Discussion about primary sources of information.

Activity: Answering questions about a primary source of information and sharing ideas.

Ways of working: Individually, in pairs and whole-class discussion to clarify thinking and gain new learning.

Suggested answers/ideas:

See Worked Example for the Starter activity.

Does not have to be topic specific.

Worked Example for the Starter activity

Challenge topic: Education for all

Starter activity: Blog as a primary source of information for learners to answer questions about.

Example website: https//www.blogtodaysschools.com

WHAT SHOULD STUDENTS BE LEARNING AT SCHOOL?

7 June 2018

Maz7918bex

I think schools haven't changed much in the last one hundred years, and they are still teaching stuff that we can now find out using a search engine. The world we live in has changed though. To start with, we didn't have technology like we do now. Schools need to start teaching skills that students need like research skills and how to deal with the amount of information thrown at us every day. They should teach more things that will help a student in real life, such as how to manage money and be a more active citizen within the community. They should also develop students' creativity and problem-solving skills so that they can do jobs in the future that computers and robots can't do.

Maria, 14

Suggested answers:

1 **a** Internet blog/response to article or letter in a newspaper or magazine

b Maria, she's 14 and we might assume she is a student at school

c 7 June 2018

d Perhaps in answer to an article about schooling today or, comments invited in answer to an internet poll to find out opinions about what schools should be teaching

e School boards, teachers, anyone in Education, other students

Main activity (approx. 20–25 mins)

Good for: Starting to analyse information gained from primary research and recording this information.

Activity: Discussion about ways of recording information gained.

Differentiation: Learners can work in pairs/small groups for support. Give choice of presentation method.

Ways of working: Individually and in pairs/small groups for support. Whole-class discussion about ways of recording information from primary research.

Different opinions/perspectives: Stress that primary research methods are a great way of gaining opinions and viewpoints from different groups of people about an issue and can form evidence as part of a perspective. For example, the information gained from teachers and students about whether school is the best place for learning can provide evidence for the perspective that 'yes, school is the best place for learning', which the learner might use as the national perspective, or 'no schools are not the best place for learning', which the learner might use for their global perspective.

Learner response and feedback: Encourage learners to work in pairs/small groups when presenting their information so they can provide continual feedback to each other.

Suggested answers/ideas: Remind learners to consider the purpose and audience for the information they have gathered. Either give learners the same presentation method or allow them to choose their own way of presenting the information gained from their questionnaire. For example, poster, leaflet, presentation (set a maximum number of slides), blog, summary, bar graph, pie chart, table.

Independent reflection activity (approx. 5–10 mins)

Good for: Encouraging learners to consider their learning from the lesson, what they think they have done well in terms of working on their own, joining in discussions, asking for help/support, helping their partner, and so on. Encourage learners to reflect on other skills as well as research skills (analysis, evaluation, reflection, communication, collaboration) they have used this lesson. This activity can be done in class, at home or in self-study time.

Getting better at research skills: Lesson 8

Lesson 8 focuses on the use of secondary information sources to gain information to help answer a research question.

CAMBRIDGE STAGE 7 RESEARCH LEARNING OBJECTIVES

1.3 Select an appropriate method and conduct research to test predictions and begin to answer a research question

1.4 Select, organise and record relevant information from a range of sources and findings from research, using appropriate methods

LEARNING GOALS

To get better at:

- understanding the difference between primary and secondary information sources
- knowing how to do an internet search to find information
- recording information gained from secondary information sources

How will I know if I reach my goals?

Good for: Learners to give examples of their learning from the lesson. They can complete the table at any point in the lesson, but they might do it at the end.

Resources needed

Learner's Skills Book 7; your own Language Support handout (if appropriate); text and Challenge topic (e.g. Education for all; see Worked Example for the Main activity).

Prior learning (approx. 5–10 mins)

Good for: Building on previous knowledge, learning and understanding. This might be from Primary Global Perspectives, from other subject areas, or from previous Global Perspectives lessons (especially Lessons 5 and 6).

Activity: Review learning about primary research and its purpose from Lesson 6.

Differentiation: Allow learners to work together for this activity. Encourage learners to come up with more words/phrases that relate to primary and/or secondary information sources to add to their lists.

Suggested answers:

a Primary: first-hand, direct, interview, questionnaire, face to face

b Secondary: indirect, reported, textbook, second-hand, existing data

c Primary are more direct, such as interviews and asking people and secondary are more book or internet based.

Not topic specific.

Starter activity (approx. 5–10 mins)

Good for: Guidance for searching for sources of information.

Activity: Putting the steps for effective secondary research in order and comparing their order with their partner's.

Ways of working: Individually, in pairs and whole-class discussion to clarify thinking and gain new learning.

Suggested answers/ideas:

C, A, E, B, D

If the internet is available in the lesson, you can model aloud the steps, doing a real search. Example search: 'School is better than home-schooling'.

Does not have to be topic specific.

Main activity (approx. 20–25 mins)

Good for: Evaluating secondary information sources to gain information to help answer a research question.

Activity: Learners answer questions about a given text (see Worked Example for the Main activity).

Differentiation: Learners can work in pairs/small groups for support. Give choice of which questions to answer to some learners. More challenging questions are: **e**, **f** and **g**. Encourage some learners to think about how they might check the reliability of the source (e.g. it lacks bias; check author and publication, date and whether the website the source is from is complete, kept updated and error-free; cross-reference the information given; check the evidence).

Ways of working: Individually and in pairs/small groups for support. Whole-class discussion about secondary sources of information.

Different opinions/perspectives: Stress that secondary research methods are a great way of gaining evidence to support a perspective. For example, for the research question, 'Is school the best place for learning to happen?' there are two clear perspectives:

- yes, school is the best place for learning to happen
- no, it is not the best place for learning to happen.

Evidence for the 'yes' perspective might come from national evidence / sources of information and evidence for the 'no' perspective might come from global evidence / sources of information.

Learner response and feedback: Encourage learners to work in pairs/small groups to give feedback to each other on the answers to the questions.

Suggested answers/ideas: See Worked Example for the Main activity.

Worked Example for the Main activity

Challenge topic: Education for all

Main activity: Secondary source of information

SCHOOLS NO LONGER PREPARE YOUNG PEOPLE FOR THE REAL WORLD

Andreas Buchanan 28/02/2019

Have you asked yourself how relevant to the real world is the History that we still study at school? Some of my friends learned about the World Wars whereas others studied the Industrial Revolution, none of which proved very useful to any of us when we left school.

Wouldn't it be better if there were more school subjects that were relevant to the real world we live in? Subjects such as finance and how to balance a household budget.

In 2017, a Stem Trust report found that some students had never carried out their own experiments in Science, relying instead on passively watching the teacher conduct the experiment and noting down what happened. Members of the Stem Trust welcomed the idea of more practical work in Science, with more field trips to museums, laboratories and research centres.

According to major computer companies such as Apple and Microsoft, more people who know how to code will be needed in the future, so information technology needs to be integrated across all subject areas, and not just taught as a separate subject in a computer laboratory once per week.

Considering all this, isn't it time that the education ministry had a complete rethink about what students should be learning in schools nowadays?

Suggested answers/ideas:

- a Schools no longer prepare young people for the real world
- b Andreas Buchanan
- c 28/02/2019
- d Education for all and that the school system needs changing to teach more relevant and useful subjects that students will be able to use in the future
- e That schools are outdated and need to teach more relevant subjects
- f Anecdotal evidence about the History that was studied and the Stem Trust report of 2017
- g Fairly convincing as it is logical and the evidence supports the argument made
- h Buchanan, A. (2019). *Schools no longer prepare young people for the real world.*

This is the only information learners have, but they would probably add the website address if this article were online and put the date they accessed the article.

Independent reflection activity (approx. 5–10 mins)

Good for: Encouraging learners to consider their learning from the lesson, what they found easy and what they needed help with. Encourage learners to reflect on other skills as well as research skills (analysis, evaluation, reflection, communication, collaboration) they have used this lesson. This activity can be done in class, at home or in self-study time.

Getting better at research skills: Lesson 9

Lesson 9 focuses on gaining information to help answer a research question. It follows on from the work done in Lesson 8.

CAMBRIDGE STAGE 7 RESEARCH LEARNING OBJECTIVES

1.2 Identify and begin to reference a range of print and multimedia sources and use them to locate relevant information and answer research questions

1.3 Select an appropriate method and conduct research to test predictions and begin to answer a research question

1.4 Select, organise and record relevant information from a range of sources and findings from research, using appropriate methods

LEARNING GOALS

To get better at:

- referencing the sources of information I use
- finding relevant information
- recording relevant information in my own words

How will I know if I reach my goals?

Good for: Learners to give examples of their learning from the lesson. They can complete the table at any point in the lesson, but they might do it at the end.

Resources needed

Learner's Skills Book 7; subject-specific words and phrases for the Starter activity; two pictures (one to show learning in school, the other to show learning at home) and accompanying websites (see Worked Example for the Main activity); Challenge topic (e.g. Education for all).

Prior learning (approx. 5 mins)

Good for: Building on previous knowledge, learning and understanding. This might be from Primary Global Perspectives, from other subject areas, or from previous Global Perspectives lessons (especially Lesson 8).

Activity: Review learning about steps to consider when using a search engine to do research.

Differentiation: Allow learners to work together for this activity. Encourage learners to come up with more steps/idea that relate to using search engines for research.

Suggested answers/ideas: Decide what information to look for; Type between three and six important key words into the search engine; Look further down the page beyond the first few results of the search; Click on the website to open it; Skim read the text: Is it easy to follow? Do I understand the text? Might it be useful? Bookmark it if so. Further ideas: Keep a list of useful websites; check the credibility of the author by searching for other articles by the author; check the reliability of the website (.org;.gov; wiki, etc.); can use videos and podcasts as well as written articles.

Not topic specific.

Starter activity (approx. 5–10 mins)

Good for: Reviewing/sharing subject-specific words and phrases for use in the lesson.

Activity: Split the class in half, give one picture to one-half of the class and a different picture to the other half of the class. For example, for topic of 'Education for all' to gain different perspectives and words/phrases: Picture 1 learning in school; Picture 2 learning at home. This could be a snowball activity (learners share in pairs, then in groups of fours and then eights to gain more words and phrases).

Suggested answers/ideas: Does not have to be topic specific, but these words and phrases will be useful during the Main activity.

Worked Example for the Starter activity

Challenge topic: Education for all

Main activity: Learners work in groups of four. For each picture, give learners a set of three relevant website addresses (see examples below) to gain information from their perspective (it's better to learn at school or it's better to learn at home). They can then use what they know about research to find one other information source. Each team member writes a summary to explain why it's best to learn at school or it's best to learn at home.

Picture ideas:

Learning at home:

- https://www.theguardian.com/education/2018/nov/03/get-to-be-free-rise-in-home-schooling
- https://www.educationotherwise.org/index.php/why-home-educate
- https://www.radionz.co.nz/national/programmes/ninetonoon/audio/2018669313/what-s-it-like-to-homeschool-your-kids

Learning at school:

- http://www.slaneylanguage.com/7-reasons-to-study-in-class-rather-than-study-alone/
- https://www.smithsonianmag.com/innovation/why-are-finlands-schools-successful-49859555/
- http://www.teaching-jobs.org/advantages-going-school-everyone-get-education/

Main activity (approx. 20–25 mins)

Good for: Evaluating secondary information sources to gain information to help answer a research question.

Activity: Learners work in groups of four. For each picture from the Starter activity, give learners a set of three relevant website addresses (see Worked Example for the Starter activity) to gain information on their picture/perspective (it's better to learn at school or it's better to learn at home). They can then use what they know about research to find one other information source. Each team member is responsible for gaining information from one website only. Give a time limit to find this information (approx. 10–15 mins). Teams come together to share their information and discuss the format they might use to persuade the other half of the class of their perspective. If time permits, teams can produce this outcome using the information they have found (podcast, presentation, video clip, leaflet, brochure, etc.) and give feedback: Did the information presented persuade them that learning is better at school or at home? How might they be better persuaded?

Differentiation: Learners work in groups of four for support and guidance. Select groups to work together or allow free choice. Give learners a choice of who researches which website address given and who finds one of the team's own.

Ways of working: Small groups for support and guidance and to develop teamworking skills.

Different opinions/perspectives: Stress that the aim of the two pictures is to give two different perspectives:

- It's better to learn at school
- It's better to learn at home.

One-half of the class finds information in small groups to persuade of the first perspective and the other half the second perspective.

Learner response and feedback: Encourage learners to give feedback to each other on the information gained. Ask questions: What did you learn? Were you persuaded by the argument?

Suggested answers/ideas: Responses will vary according to picture and websites given.

Independent reflection activity; Self-assessment; Challenge topic review (approx. 15–20 mins)

Good for: Encouraging learners to consider their learning and progression in learning in lessons. Ask them to be as honest as they can. There is no correct response. Encourage learners to reflect on other skills as well as research skills (analysis, evaluation, reflection, communication, collaboration) they have used this lesson, for example, collaboration skills as they worked in teams.

Learners also complete the self-assessment to set their own learning targets. Learners look back at previous self-assessment and think about and shade where they think they are at this time in their learning. 'With help' refers to guidance given (pointing a learner in the right direction, although examples should still come from the learner), for example, from you, other learners, previous work done by the learner in Learner's Skills Book 7. For the Challenge topic review, learners explore the topic used in this section to develop research skills. These activities can be done in class, at home or in self-study time.

Suggested examples:

1.1 *Construct relevant research questions.* Features of a good research question: a question that people care about; a question that is not too broad, too narrow or too vague; a question that allows for information to be found/an answer. Good research questions: 'Is home-schooling better than learning at school?' 'Do humans need animals for survival?'

1.2 *Identify and begin to reference a range of print and multimedia sources and use them to locate relevant information and answer research questions.* To acknowledge/recognise someone else's ideas: Wiggins (2016). *Students Learn Best When You Do This.* Teachthought [online] Available at: https://www.teachthought.com/pedagogy/students-learn-best (Accessed 2/12/2019).

1.3 *Select an appropriate method and conduct research to test predictions and begin to answer a research question.* Any example steps: Decide what information I need to look for; Type between three and six important key words into the search engine; Look further down the page beyond the first few results of the search; Click on the website to open it; Skim read the text: Is it easy to follow? Do I understand the text? Might it be useful? Bookmark it if so.

1.4 *Select, organise and record relevant information from a range of sources and findings from research, using appropriate methods.* Any relevant example. Learners can use examples from their Learner's Skills Book 7 from Lesson 9. They can write the source and a sentence or two from it in their own words. Ask them to check that the information is:

- clearly worded
- relates to the topic
- relates to the question
- does not contain words from the source.

Section 2 Analysis

Introduction

The learning objectives and learning goals for analysis skills for Stage 7 focus on the following:

- Identifying perspectives
- Interpreting data
- Making connections
- Solving problems

However, you might also find opportunities within the lessons to develop some of the other Global Perspectives skills. For example, when identifying ideas and evidence from different perspectives, not only will learners be developing analysis skills, they will also be developing their research skills.

The ideas given in this Teacher's Book 7 are suggestions only, and the activities can be used with any of the Global Perspectives Challenge topics for Stages 7 to 9, although Worked Examples are provided for some learning activities. It is hoped that the ideas in this Teacher's Book 7 will help you structure your lessons in an active learning way with input from you as the teacher to help guide and support learners to become more effective at being able to analyse issues and suggest courses of action to help resolve these issues.

Analysis skills overview

Learning objectives	2.1 Identify ideas and evidence from different perspectives within different sources on a given topic 2.2 Explain how graphical or numerical data supports an argument 2.3 Explain causes of a local or global issue and the consequences on others 2.4 Suggest and justify different actions to make a positive difference to a national or global issue
Challenge topic ideas	Globalisation; Education for all; Humans and other species; Disease and health; Sport and recreation; Conflict and peace
Key points	• Understanding that a cause is responsible for a situation or issue and a consequence is the result of a situation or issue • Confusion between the terms 'issue' and 'perspectives' • Confusion between the terms 'perspective' and 'opinion' and 'viewpoint' • Understanding the difference between a global, national, local and personal perspective • A perspective is a way of looking at something, based on evidence. An opinion is what someone thinks and is often unsupported • Evidence can be in the form of graphs, photos, video clips, audio recordings and written texts (newspaper/magazine articles, books, leaflets, newsletters, blogs, etc.) • A course of action should relate to the issue. A local issue often needs a local course of action

<table>
<tr><td>Language support</td><td>

- Pre-teach key vocabulary: cause; consequence; issue, perspective; local; national; global; personal; cultural; double-bar graph; title, axis, labels, scale, bars; prediction; conclusion; identify; explain; resources; evaluate; course of action; solution; stakeholder; vested interest; conclusion. Also include any topic-specific vocabulary for the Challenge topics – Globalisation; Education for all; Humans and other species; Disease and health; Sport and recreation; Conflict and peace.
- Handout of words/phrases signalling cause and consequence and examples of their use:
  - Signalling causes – because, due to, since, as, so/as long as … , now that
  - Signalling consequences – as a result, therefore, that's why, so, consequently, this means, this leads to, for this reason, due to this, if … then.

</td></tr>
<tr><td>Cross-skills links</td><td>

1 **Research**

1.2 Identify and begin to reference a range of print and multimedia sources and use them to locate relevant information and answer research questions.

1.3 Select an appropriate method and conduct research to test predictions and begin to answer a research question.

1.4 Select, organise and record relevant information from a range of sources and findings from research, using appropriate methods.

3 **Evaluation**

3.1 Evaluate sources, considering the author and purpose, recognising that some sources may be biased.

3.2 Discuss the effectiveness of a source, making explicit reference to its development of an argument.

4 **Reflection**

4.3 Consider ways that personal perspective on an issue may have changed as a result of conducting research or exploring different perspectives.

4.4 Identify skills learned or improved during an activity and relate to personal strengths and areas for improvement.

5 **Collaboration**

5.1 The team assign roles and divide tasks fairly, considering the skills of team members and time available, and work together to achieve a shared outcome.

5.2 The team member introduces useful ideas to help achieve a shared outcome and works positively to resolve conflict, solve problems and encourage other team members to participate, when required.

6 **Communication**

6.1 Present information and arguments clearly with some reasoning, referencing sources where appropriate.

6.2 Listen to ideas and information and offer relevant and well-judged contributions that demonstrate understanding of the issue.

</td></tr>
</table>

Starting with analysis skills: Lesson 1

Lesson 1 focuses on identifying what the term 'analysis' means and identifying the causes and consequences of situations/issues.

CAMBRIDGE STAGE 7 ANALYSIS LEARNING OBJECTIVES

2.3 Explain causes of a local or global issue and the consequences on others

LEARNING GOALS

To start to:

- understand what the term 'analysis' means
- identify how to analyse something
- make notes of relevant information in my own words

How will I know if I reach my goals?

Good for: Learners to give examples of their learning from the lesson. They can complete the table at any point in the lesson, but they might do it at the end.

Resources needed

Learner's Skills Book 7; your own Language Support handout (if appropriate); Challenge topic, e.g. Globalisation – (see Worked Example for the Starter and Main activities); four or more pictures and a list of questions, all about the same topic (two copies of each; see Worked Example for the Starter and Main Activities); internet access; computers.

Prior learning (approx. 5 mins)

Good for: Building on previous knowledge, learning and understanding. This might be from Primary Global Perspectives for the starter activity, or from other subject areas. It asks learners to produce words/phrases related to the picture(s) and for use in the next activities.

Activity: Find out what words/phrases learners already know to be able to analyse the picture in the Starter activity.

Differentiation: Learners work in pairs and then share with another pair to gain further ideas (they need to have the same picture).

Suggested ideas: Use four or more different pictures (see Worked Example for the Main activity for ideas) to do with the same topic as learners will work in groups with one of the pictures in the starter and main activities. Each picture can be copied twice and given to two different pairs to enable sharing for this activity.

Not topic specific but see Worked Example .

Starter activity (approx. 10 mins)

Good for: Enabling learners to start thinking about what it means to analyse something (causes and consequences).

Activity: Using words/phrases from their Prior learning activity, learners complete the text about their picture.

Ways of working: In pairs or small-group work to complete the text/paragraph about the picture.

Suggested answers: Any reasonable and relevant response, depending on the pictures/topic. See Worked Example for the Starter and Main activities.

Main activity (approx. 20–25 mins)

Good for: Gaining further information to analyse a picture, explaining in more detail the causes and consequences of a situation or issue.

Activity: Give each small group a series of questions. Each member of the group chooses one question to research to add to the information about their picture from the Starter activity. Give a specific time for research. Learners share their information and produce a transcript and recorded commentary or their picture (situation/issue, causes and consequences). Use some of the recorded commentaries as a listening activity with learners making notes about the other pictures.

Differentiation: Group work to support. Choice of questions. Choice of suitable websites.

Ways of working: In groups to do individual research and then join together to share information and write a transcript and commentary. Whole-class listening to commentaries and recording information about each of the pictures (situation, causes, consequences, other relevant information).

Different opinions/perspectives: Encourage learners to look at their picture from different perspectives. For example, the viewpoint of the people in the picture, the perspective of the country where the situation is taking place, the global perspective and the learners' own perspectives about the situation (particularly after they have done their research) – the focus of Lesson 2.

Learner response and feedback: Encourage learners to focus on their question for the research. They should also explain the information they found to their teammates and answer any questions their teammates have. Listen to each other as they write their transcript and record their commentary for their picture.

Suggested answers/ideas: See Worked Example for the Starter and Main activities.

Worked Example for Starter and Main activities

Challenge topic: Globalisation

Suggested pictures:

- 'Sweatshop' factory with workers (clothes; mobile phones)
- Ploughing by hand (rice farmers)
- Workers in a tea plantation
- Workers loading tree trunks onto a truck
- Farm workers harvesting salad, spinach, peppers or fruit picking.

Questions for each group:

1 What is happening in the picture? Where do you think this is?

2 Why do you think the situation in the picture is happening?

3 What do you think the people in that country think about the situation in the picture?

4 What happens/might happen as a result of the situation in the picture?

5 What do you think about the situation in the picture?

Learners can choose which question they research or you can give each learner in a group a specific question.

For example:

Situation: Sweatshop factory with workers making clothes

1 People are working in a sweatshop making clothes / there are lots of people in not very good working conditions, possibly in ...

2 There is a demand for cheap clothes around the world.

3 They need to earn a living.

4 Someone could get hurt if machinery isn't working properly.

5 I think ...

Independent reflection activity (approx. 5–10 mins)

Good for: Learners to give examples of what they have found the most difficult in the lesson. This might be skill or content specific, for example, finding information to answer their question; working in a team because no one really knew what they were doing/there were no roles or the team lacked organisation, and so on. Encourage learners to reflect on other skills as well as analysis skills (research, evaluation, reflection, communication, collaboration) they have used this lesson. This activity can be done in class, at home or in self-study time.

Starting with analysis skills: Lesson 2

Lesson 2 focuses on understanding the difference between an issue and a perspective.

CAMBRIDGE STAGE 7 ANALYSIS LEARNING OBJECTIVES

2.1 Identify ideas and evidence from different perspectives within different sources on a given topic

LEARNING GOALS

To start to:

- understand what an issue is
- understand what a perspective is
- identify an issue
- identify a perspective

How will I know if I reach my goals?

Good for: Learners to give examples of their learning from the lesson. They can complete the table at any point in the lesson, but they might do it at the end.

Resources needed

Learner's Skills Book 7; your own Language Support handout (if appropriate); Challenge topic, e.g. Globalisation; text (written, audio or video) for the topic (see the Worked Example for the Main activity).

Prior learning (approx. 5 mins)

Good for: Building on previous knowledge, learning and understanding. This might be from Primary Global Perspectives, from other subject areas and from their last Global Perspectives lesson.

Activity: Ask learners to consider the work done in Lesson 1 and write down the words/phrases they used to signal causes and consequences. For example, 'because' is used to say why something has happened (cause).

Differentiation: Give learners a list of words/phrases and ask them to put them into two lists: words/phrases that signal causes and those that signal consequences. Learners work in pairs.

Suggested answers:

1 Causes – because, due to, since, as, so long as … , as long as … , now that

2 Consequences – as a result, therefore, that's why, so, consequently, this means, this leads to, for this reason, due to this, if … then

Not topic specific. Learners will be using these words/phrases in subsequent lessons.

Starter activity (approx. 5 mins)

Good for: Starting to see the difference between an issue and a perspective about an issue.

Activity: Learners decide which words relate to issues and which to perspectives.

Ways of working: Individually, in pairs and whole-class discussion to explore understanding of the different between an issue and a perspective.

Suggested answers:

1 **Issues:** poverty, homelessness, crime, pollution, globalisation

Perspectives: global, national, local, personal, cultural

2 a An issue is an important topic or problem for debate or discussion. An issue often needs a course of action to help resolve it.

b A perspective is a way of looking at something.

Main activity (approx. 20–25 mins)

Good for: Identifying issues and perspectives from a text to help clarify understanding of the difference. For task 2, the three further issues and perspectives do not need to come from the text.

Activity: Learners identify issues and perspectives from the text. The text can be written, audio or a video clip – see Worked Example for the Main activity.

Differentiation: Text lengths can vary, or a video clip might be suitable. Learners can refer to their definitions of an 'issue' and a 'perspective'. Learners can read the text as a class and highlight issues and perspectives in two different colours. Then class discussion.

Ways of working: Individually, in pairs, whole class to share ideas, clarify own thinking/understanding.

Different opinions/perspectives: The lesson is about encouraging learners to see examples of different perspectives.

Learner response and feedback: Learners ask each other why they have underlined/noted what they have. Encourage learners to look at the definitions of perspective and issue to give feedback.

Suggested answers:

1 These will vary according to the text.

2 Further issues – anything that might need a solution/course of action; perspectives – ways of looking at issues. For example, perspectives might come from farmers, politicians, families, tourists, artists, environmentalists, nutritionists, and so on.

Worked Example for the Main activity

Challenge topic: Globalisation: Issues and perspectives

Resource for Lesson 2: Text about globalisation to identify issues and perspectives

THE ADVANTAGES AND DISADVANTAGES OF GLOBALISATION

Nowadays, no matter how far apart we all live, we are all connected. Many people look for jobs in other countries because these countries need a skilled workforce to develop. The money that workers earn and spend in these countries helps that country move forward, and more jobs benefit workers and their families. Of the approximate 7 billion people living on this planet, about 200 million are migrants, which means cities are vibrant mixes of cultures, noticeable in the many types of food available.

Young people interact with others living in different countries by playing online games and communicating via social media, which helps them feel connected and gain different opinions and viewpoints about things happening in the world. All over the world, young people are wearing the same things, influenced by popular brands, identifiable by their logos. Young people listen to the same songs, sometimes not understanding them, but listening anyway, because they know their peers across the world are listening to them. They feel connected through fashion, music and trends like going to the same fast-food restaurants, present in every city around the world, whether in China or New Zealand. That's good for the owners of these restaurants, not so good for the health of a nation.

There's no doubt that where globalisation has meant quicker economic growth; there has been an improvement in living standards and a reduction in the amount of poverty. An improved living standard leads to improved health and longer life expectancy.

Environmentalists report improved awareness about caring for the planet by polluting less and recycling more, but are concerned about globalisation depleting the Earth's natural resources. Businesses also benefit from improved technology, although technological advancements are creating unemployment for workers in traditional jobs like manufacturing.

For countries that haven't been able to benefit from globalisation, the gap between rich and poor is growing, with the number of people below the poverty on the increase. Health agencies worry about the increase in international travel, which could spread diseases, and the older generation think culture is becoming a thing of the past as more traditions and local languages start to disappear.

Suggested answers:

- **Issues:** Poverty, unemployment, loss of language and culture, loss of natural resources, spread of disease
- **Perspectives:** Young people, workers and their families, health agencies, environmentalists, older generation, businesses, fast-food restaurant owners

Independent reflection (approx. 5–10 mins)

Good for: Encouraging learners to consider what they found easy during the lesson. Ask them to be as honest as they can. There is no correct response and they can choose more than one option. Encourage explanation but not all learners will be able to do this. Encourage learners to reflect on other skills as well as analysis skills (research, evaluation, reflection, communication, collaboration) they have used this lesson. This activity can be done in class, at home or in self-study time.

Starting with analysis skills: Lesson 3

Lesson 3 focuses on further understanding of what a perspective is and how to analyse data.

CAMBRIDGE STAGE 7 ANALYSIS LEARNING OBJECTIVES

2.1 Identify ideas and evidence from different perspectives within different sources on a given topic

2.2 Explain how graphical or numerical data supports an argument

LEARNING GOALS

To start to:

- understand what a perspective is
- identify important information from a graph
- understand the importance of graphs as evidence

How will I know if I reach my goals?

Good for: Learners to give examples of their learning from the lesson. They can complete the table at any point in the lesson, but they might do it at the end.

Resources needed

Learner's Skills Book 7; your own Language Support handout (if appropriate); picture and list of people for Prior learning activity (see below); graph and questions (see below, including Worked Example for the Starter activity); Challenge topic (e.g. 'Globalisation'); set of data for the Main activity (see below).

Prior learning (approx. 5 mins)

Good for: Building on previous knowledge, learning and understanding. This might be from Primary Global Perspectives, from other subject areas, or from previous Global Perspectives lessons.

Activity: Show all learners the same picture (e.g. picture of a sweatshop or other picture used in Lesson 1). Also give them a list of four different types of people who might react to the picture (e.g. Workers, Families, Factory owners, (Health agencies) Doctor, Children, schools).

Differentiation: Learners work in pairs. Discuss responses in class.

Suggested answers/ideas: Any reasonable and relevant response. For example, Workers might appreciate that they can work to earn money to feed their families, but health agencies might fear that the working conditions are dangerous. The idea is to stimulate learners' own ideas and reinforce work done on different perspectives in Lesson 2.

Not topic specific.

Starter activity (approx. 10–15 mins)

Good for: Analysing data and exploring bar graphs so that learners can create their own in the Main activity.

Activity: Show learners data in a graph format and hand out related questions (see Worked Example for the Starter activity). They use the graph to answer the questions. They can work individually or in pairs. Class discussion to go through answers.

Differentiation: Write four more of their own questions.

Suggested answers/ideas: See Worked Example for the Starter activity.

Any topic can be used.

Worked Example for the Starter activity

Challenge topic: Globalisation

Bar graph showing which company logos are the most memorable to people in the United States and the United Kingdom.

	Nike	Apple	McDonalds	Coca Cola	Google	Microsoft	Amazon	Other
■ USA	20	14	10	7	2.5	3	1.5	42
■ UK	17.5	17	15	10	3	1.5	1.5	34.5

Questions to ask:

1 Which is the second most memorable named logo in the UK?

2 Which is the least memorable logo in the USA?

3 What percentage of people asked in the UK said that McDonalds was the most memorable logo?

4 Which logo is the most memorable in both countries?

5 Apart from Nike, which logo is more memorable in the USA than in the UK?

6 Which logo is equally memorable in the USA and in the UK?

Answers:

1	Apple	4	Nike
2	Amazon	5	Microsoft
3	15%	6	Amazon

Further questions which learners might come up with:

- Is Coca Cola more memorable in the UK or the USA? This type of question can be asked of any of the logos.
- What percentage of people asked in the USA said that Google had the most memorable logo? This type of question can be asked of any company and country.
- Is the Apple logo more memorable than the McDonalds logo? This type of question can be asked of any of the logos.

Main activity (approx. 20–25 mins)

Good for: Recording research findings.

Activity: Give learners a set of data. You can create this in class and base it on the same topic as the Starter activity. For example, ask learners to put their hands up to tell you which logo is the most memorable for them (Nike, Apple, McDonalds, Coca Cola, Google, Microsoft and Amazon). You can divide the data by gender.

Model how to create a double-bar graph using key terms for the five parts of a graph (title, axis, labels, scale, bars). Explain that these parts each help to interpret the data/information.

1 Before creating a graph, learners write predictions based on the data, for example:

   I predict the most memorable .... will be ....

   I predict the least memorable .... will be ....

   I predict that boys will think that .... is more memorable than ....

   I predict that most of my classmates will not have heard of ....

2 Learners create a double-bar graph as in the Worked Example for the set of data given to them. For a double-bar graph, they need to divide the data by gender (boys/girls).

3 Learners check their predictions. Ask them to answer the questions.

Differentiation: Learners can work individually and share in pairs once complete or work in pairs and share in fours. Model how to create a (double) bar graph for task 2. Some learners can write a conclusive statement that can be supported by their data. For example, 'Everyone in the class thinks that Nike has the most memorable logo'.

Ways of working: In pairs for support and to clarify own thinking. Whole-class feedback on the presentation of the data and the importance of this data as evidence.

Different opinions/perspectives: Stress that presenting data in a graph is a good way of presenting different viewpoints/opinions on a topic. Graphs are especially useful for presenting information gained from primary research.

Learner response and feedback: It doesn't matter that learners find creating graphs a challenge. A graph might not be a suitable way of presenting data, but learners should know that it's one of the ways of presenting evidence to support an argument or a perspective. They can also just summarise their findings as a paragraph. Use peer feedback so learners can clarify their own understanding and gain ideas from their peers.

Suggested answers: Answers will vary as different learners will predict different outcomes from their graphs. Graphs should look similar if the same data is used. Learners can explore how and why any graphs look different.

Independent reflection activity; Self-assessment; Challenge topic review (approx. 15–20 mins)

Good for: Encouraging learners to consider their learning in lessons. Encourage learners to reflect on other skills as well as analysis skills (research, evaluation, reflection, communication, collaboration) they have used this lesson – for example, communication skills as they created a graph to communicate research findings.

Learners also complete the self-assessment to set their own learning targets before they move on. Learners think about and shade where they think they are at this time in their learning. 'With help' refers to guidance given (pointing a learner in the right direction, although examples should still come from the learner), for example, from you, other learners, previous work done by the learner in the Learner's Skills Book 7. For the Challenge topic review, learners explore the topic used in this section to develop analysis skills. These activities can be done in class, at home or in self-study time.

Suggested examples:

2.1 *Identify ideas and evidence from different perspectives within different sources, on a given topic.* Learners give examples of issues and perspectives (global, national, local, personal and cultural); an issue is often a problem that needs solving; a perspective is a worldview (stemming from upbringing or research about an issue); evidence for a perspective (worldview) can be from different groups of people/organisations.

2.2 *Explain how graphical or numerical data supports an argument.* Graphical or numerical data can be used as evidence to test a prediction.

2.3 *Explain causes of a local or global issue and the consequences on others.* Analysis is looking deeper at an issue, not just describing the issue but also what might have caused it and what might happen as a result of it.

Developing analysis skills: Lesson 4

Lesson 4 focuses on problem-solving skills and some basic steps to approaching issues that need resolving. It follows on from work done in Lesson 1 on the causes and consequences of issues.

CAMBRIDGE STAGE 7 ANALYSIS LEARNING OBJECTIVES

2.4 Suggest and justify different actions to make a positive difference to a national or global issue

LEARNING GOALS

To develop knowledge and understanding about:

- basic problem-solving steps
- how to approach resolving an issue

How will I know if I reach my goals?

Good for: Learners to give examples of their learning from the lesson. They can complete the table at any point in the lesson, but they might do it at the end.

Resources needed

Learner's Skills Book 7; your own Language Support handout (if appropriate); Challenge topic (e.g. 'Globalisation') and list of issues (see Worked Example for the Main activity).

Prior learning (approx. 5–10 mins)

Good for: Building on previous knowledge, learning and understanding. This might be from Primary Global Perspectives, from other subject areas, or from previous Stage 7 Global Perspectives lessons.

Activity: Using the text 'The advantages and disadvantages of globalisation' from Lesson 2, learners review all the issues that might need resolving.

Differentiation: Allow learners to look back in their Learner's Skills Book 7. Some will not need to. Learners can work in pairs for support.

Suggested answers/ideas: Any reasonable and relevant response, but responses will be from the text used.

Not necessarily topic specific. You can ask learners to brainstorm a list of issues in their groups and share with the class.

Starter activity (approx. 10 mins)

Good for: Getting learners to think about problem-solving strategies and how to approach coming up with a course of action to help resolve an issue.

Activity: Learners put the problem-solving steps in order.

Ways of working: Individually, in pairs and whole-class discussion.

Suggested answers:

E (What is the issue? It is important that learners understand that it is something that has a course of action to help resolve it.)

B (For whom is it an issue? Why is it an issue?)

A (What information do I need? Where do I get this information? Primary and/or secondary research sources?)

D (Is my course of action realistic? What do I need to implement it?)

F (Who does what and when?)

C (Does my course of action help resolve the issue?)

Not topic specific.

Main activity (approx. 20–25 mins)

Good for: Exploring a strategy to help resolve issues and getting learners to plan.

Activity: Give learners a list of issues to choose from (issues could be based on a specific topic or problems that learners are familiar with and are personal to them). They choose an issue and complete the table in the Learner's Skills Book 7. First model with a basic example, for example:

Problem/Issue: When should I do homework?

Possible answer 1: Straight after school every day

Reasons for/against: I have swimming three times a week after school

Possible answer 2: Saturdays

Reasons for/against: I need a day off from school

Elicit possible answer 3 and reasons from learners.

See Worked Example for topic-specific example.

Discussion how learners found this strategy. Did it help them understand problem-solving a bit more?

Differentiation: Learners can work in pairs for support. They could use a graphic organiser/table to organise thoughts.

Ways of working: Individually or in pairs to share ideas, clarify own thinking. Whole-class discussion about problem-solving strategies.

Different opinions/perspectives: Encourage learners to consider different levels of help/action: global, national, local and personal.

Learner response and feedback: Encourage learners to evaluate each other's courses of action. Are they realistic? (doable, don't cost much, not too large-scale?) Will they work? Do they relate to the issue?

Suggested answers: These depend on the issues given/chosen.

Worked Example for the Main activity

Challenge topic: Globalisation

Problem/Issue: What can we do about the loss of local language and traditions?

Possible course of action 1: Poster persuading of the importance of local languages and traditions.

Reasons for/against: Easy to do as an individual or in pairs; time to make poster; resources for poster.

Other factors: Where to put the poster? How many posters? How large? What to say on the poster? What language to write the poster in?

Possible course of action 2: Persuade the Head Teacher to hold a language and traditions awareness day after school, during the school day or at the weekend.

Reasons for/against: Can invite parents, local community, reach a wide audience; get the school interested; would take time for planning, a day of not having lessons, or a weekend day.

Other factors: Who to involve? Who does what? When to organise it for? Resources needed?

Possible course of action 3: A presentation promoting the importance of local languages and traditions in a school gathering.

Reasons for/against: Can be done individually or in small groups, in class. Date and time for the gathering needed.

Other factors: Need permissions (Class teacher and Head Teacher), Decide on who presents what, resources needed for the presentation.

Independent reflection activity (approx. 5–10 mins)

Good for: Encouraging learners to consider their learning from the lesson about whether they feel more able to come up with ideas to resolve issues. Encourage learners to reflect on other skills as well as analysis skills (research, evaluation, reflection, communication, collaboration) they have used this lesson. This activity can be done in class, at home or in self-study time.

Developing analysis skills: Lesson 5

Lesson 5 focuses on identifying information from a national perspective. It follows on from the work done in Lesson 2 on the difference between issues and perspectives.

CAMBRIDGE STAGE 7 ANALYSIS LEARNING OBJECTIVES

2.1 Identify ideas and evidence from different perspectives within different sources on a given topic

LEARNING GOALS

To develop knowledge and understanding about:

- the difference between a national and a personal perspective
- how different information sources contain different perspectives
- to identify a national perspective in a source of information

How will I know if I reach my goals?

Good for: Learners to give examples of their learning from the lesson. They can complete the table at any point in the lesson, but they might do it at the end.

Resources needed

Learner's Skills Book 7; your own Language Support handout (if appropriate); two pictures for the Starter activity (see below); Challenge topic (e.g. 'Globalisation', but any topic is suitable) and text (see Worked Example for the Main activity).

Prior learning (approx. 5–10 mins)

Good for: Building on previous knowledge, learning and understanding. This might be from Primary Global Perspectives, from other subject areas, or from previous Global Perspectives lessons (Lesson 2).

Activity: Review learning from Lesson 2: Learners write initial definitions of what they think a national and a personal perspective are. They can come back to this at the end of the lesson to make any amendments or add anything.

Differentiation: Allow learners to look back in their Learner's Skills Book 7. Some will not need to. Learners work in pairs and then share ideas with the whole class.

Suggested answers: Any reasonable and relevant response.

A national perspective relates to a specific country and is evident by what people think/believe about something (possibly due to culture and traditions), and is based on the needs and issues of the whole country.

A personal perspective is what an individual thinks about something depending on their upbringing/ education and what they have learned from various sources throughout their life to form their perspective.

Starter activity (approx. 10 mins)

Good for: Discussion about a positive and a negative perspective. Can also be used for consequences (positive and negative).

Activity: Show learners two pictures, for example:

A Negative perspective about globalisation: https://bizfluent.com/info-8564715-negative-impacts-globalization-environment.html

(e.g. pollution, overexploitation of resources, urbanisation, loss of culture and tradition as everywhere looks the same)

B Positive perspective about globalisation: https://opinionfront.com/positive-effects-of-globalization

(e.g. alternative energy sources for sustainability, people connecting across countries for business and pleasure, sharing cultures and traditions)

Learners identify which of the two pictures shows a positive perspective and give reasons why and which shows a negative perspective and give reasons why.

Ways of working: Individually, in pairs and whole-class discussion.

Suggested answers: Depends on pictures given.

Not topic specific.

Main activity (approx. 20–25 mins)

Good for: Identifying ideas and evidence from a national perspective.

Activity: Discussion about identifying a national perspective and ideas in the text. The Worked Example for the Main activity uses a written text on a national perspective from one particular country, but any country can be used, and the text can be in any form.

Differentiation: Learners can work in pairs for support. They can look back at their Prior learning activity for the lesson to establish what is meant by a national perspective.

Ways of working: Individually and in pairs to share ideas, clarify own thinking. Whole class discussion about ideas in the text.

Different opinions/perspectives: Learners are exploring a national perspective.

Learner response and feedback: Encourage learners to discuss in pairs / as a class the ideas in the text.

Suggested answers: Learners are developing their ability to identify different perspectives. Answers depend on the text used.

Worked Example for the Main activity

Challenge topic: Globalisation

GLOBALISATION – DIFFERENT PERSPECTIVES

Some argue that globalisation has a negative effect on the daily lives of people around the world. However, in some parts of the world, globalisation has improved the daily lives of people in many ways. One of these improvements is through the use of internet technology in daily communications and interactions, thereby reducing isolation, especially amongst the older generation.

People here feel positively about globalisation as it highlights human rights activities across the world through increased access to media sources. Due to technology, globalisation has the ability to reach all areas of the world in a very short space of time. As a result of this highly interconnected world, not only can people draw attention to human rights violations, they can use social media to promote human rights issues to the world.

Another positive feature of globalisation is within the education system. Traditionally, education was seen as face to face at a fixed time and place, with a teacher and students in a classroom, and if people wanted to find information, they went to libraries. This is no longer the case, as technology has enabled education online, meaning that students can access information via their mobile phone. This is changing the education system here as in many countries because those that can't afford to attend school, or who live too far away from their nearest school, can access lessons via their mobile phone.

Another, perhaps previously unthought-of benefit of globalisation is simply gaining an awareness of how important education for all is, partly due to migration increasing the motivation to gain a good education.

Suggested answers:

1 Globalisation is positive/brings benefits such as education for all, interconnectedness and increased awareness of human rights issues.

2 No correct response. Ideas include: promote human rights; technology, access to media sources, highly interconnected, and so on.

3 Isolation amongst the elderly; Human rights (violations and promotion of); Education for all (education too expensive; schools too far from where students live).

4 Highlights human rights activities globally through increased access to media; highly interconnected world; education system changing because of technology and awareness about the importance of education due to migration. (Encourage learners to look for the words/phrases that signal causes – because, due to, since, as, so long as … , as long as … , now that.)

5 Reduced isolation (amongst the elderly); draw attention to human rights violations and promote human rights issues; enables education online; students can access information via their mobile phones; awareness about the importance of education. (Encourage learners to look for the words/phrases that signal consequences – as a result, therefore, that's why, so, consequently, this means, this leads to, for this reason, due to this, if … then.)

6 It is positive, as it only highlights the benefits of globalisation for this country. No disadvantages are mentioned.

Independent reflection activity (approx. 5–10 mins)

Good for: Encouraging learners to reflect on what helped them learn this lesson and how they helped someone else learn. This activity can be done in class, at home or in self-study time.

Developing analysis skills: Lesson 6

Lesson 6 focuses on distinguishing information which comes from a global and a national perspective.

CAMBRIDGE STAGE 7 ANALYSIS LEARNING OBJECTIVES

2.1 Identify ideas and evidence from different perspectives within different sources on a given topic

LEARNING GOALS

To develop knowledge and understanding about:

- the difference between a national and a global perspective
- how different information sources contain different perspectives
- identifying a global perspective in a source of information

How will I know if I reach my goals?

Good for: Learners to give examples of their learning from the lesson. They can complete the table at any point in the lesson, but they might do it at the end.

Resources needed

Learner's Skills Book 7; your own Language Support handout (if appropriate); a picture for the Starter activity (see below); Challenge topic (e.g. ' Globalisation'), list of websites and access to internet (see Worked Example for the Main activity below).

Prior learning (approx. 5–10 mins)

Good for: Building on previous knowledge, learning and understanding. This might be from Primary Global Perspectives, from other subject areas, or from previous Stage 7 Global Perspectives lessons.

Activity: Review learning to start to think about formulating a personal perspective about the topic. Encourage learners to give reasons why their personal perspective might have changed/developed. Personal perspectives are covered more in Section 4 'Reflection'.

Differentiation: Allow learners to look back in their Learner's Skills Book 7. Some will not need to. Learners can work in pairs for support. Some may not be able to give reasons.

Suggested answers: Any reasonable and relevant response. For example, learners might say that they used to think globalisation was a good thing and now they don't because of the information they gained from different perspectives in the different sources on, for example, the case study of sweatshops in Bangladesh.

Starter activity (approx. 10–15 mins)

Good for: Stimulating thinking about a global and a national perspective.

Activity (approx. 10–15 mins): Show learners a picture on a globalisation topic, for example:

- a cartoon of someone asking where the information desk is, with the response that it has been relocated to another country (National perspective, as many national/local companies move to places where wages are not so high making it more inconvenient for people in that country/locality) https://www.coe.int/en/web/compass/globalisation
- a picture of McDonalds logo (Global perspective as everyone around the world can access McDonalds or similar, e.g. Starbucks, Amazon, Nike).

Learners decide whether the picture explores a national or a global perspective and give reasons why they think the way they do.

Ways of working: Individually, in pairs and whole-class discussion.

Suggested answers: Depends on picture given. No correct answer but reasoning is important.

A global perspective may come from a specific country, organisation, institution or even an individual, but it will have influence that spreads beyond any one country.

A national perspective is based on the needs of the whole country.

Main activity (approx. 20–25 mins)

Good for: Distinguishing between sources of information that present a global and a national perspective or a mixture of both.

Activity: Give learners a list of website addresses (see Worked Example for the Main activity). Ask them to review each website and decide whether they think the information comes from a global or a national perspective or both. Class discussion to explore the difference between a global and a national perspective. Learners then choose one of the websites or you can give them one. They write the main idea, the perspective the information comes from, whether they agree with this perspective or not and why.

Differentiation: Learners can work in pairs for support. Give each pair/small group just one or two websites to explore and decide whether the information is from a global or a national perspective. Refer learners to the key terms and 'Tips' in their Learner's Skills Book 7 for definitions about global and national perspectives.

Ways of working: Pairs to share ideas, clarify own thinking and as support.

Different opinions/perspectives: The activity focuses on the understanding of information from different perspectives within different information sources.

Learner response and feedback: Encourage learners to give feedback to each other by asking questions: What is the main idea? How do you know the information is from a global/national perspective? Do you agree with this perspective? Why? Why not?

Suggested answers: Answers will vary. Remind learners how to determine a national and global perspective:

- **A global perspective** may come from a specific country, organisation, institution or even an individual but it will have influence that spreads beyond any one country. For example: 'Globalisation has more benefits than disadvantages globally.'
- **A national perspective** is based on the needs of a whole country. For example, 'Without globalisation, we would not be as economically developed as we now are and more people would be living in poverty.'

Worked Example for the Main activity

Challenge topic: Globalisation

1 List of possible website addresses:

A http://fairtrade.com.au/Fairtrade-in-Action/Sustainable-Development (global perspective and also national perspective – Fairtrade is global and this branch represents Australia and New Zealand)

B https://www.un.org/sustainabledevelopment/sustainable-development-goals (global perspective – United Nations website)

C Globalization Explained in One Minute https://www.youtube.com/watch?v=Xc0bR9tiDyU (global perspective)

D India & Globalisation https://www.youtube.com/watch?v=i_ntVgNP604 (national perspective – case study from India)

E Making globalisation work: Better lives for all https://www.youtube.com/watch?v=UO4r1KEDl1Q (global perspective)

F Hidden Face of Globalization (Part II) https://www.youtube.com/watch?v=a0IBM7_BvTw (national perspective – Bangladesh)

G Globalization in Singapore https://www.youtube.com/watch?v=m2unVhu6J5E (national perspective – Singapore welcomes people from all over the world to study and work)

Suggested answer:

3 Choose one of the websites. For one piece of information/evidence from that website, write a sentence or short paragraph to tell someone else: https://www.youtube.com/watch?v=UO4r1KEDl1Q

a The main idea: Globalisation is not new, but the effects have become greater with many benefits for society.

b The perspective(s) given: A global perspective.

c Your opinion of the perspective(s) including why you do / do not agree with it: Example: I think there are more disadvantages than benefits, for example, every city is starting to look the same and local and national culture is disappearing.

Independent reflection activity; Self-assessment; Challenge topic review (approx. 15–20 mins)

Good for: Encouraging learners to consider their learning and progression in learning in lessons. Ask them to be as honest as they can. Encourage learners to think about how they can further develop their understanding of the differences between global, national and personal perspectives, for example, by asking you or their peers or coming up with examples of their own.

Learners also complete the self-assessment to set their own learning targets before they move on. Learners think about and shade where they think they are at this time in their learning. 'With help' refers to guidance given (pointing a learner in the right direction, although examples should still come from the learner), for example, from you, other learners, previous work done by the learner in the Learner's Skills Book 7. For the Challenge topic review, learners explore the topic used in this section to develop analysis skills. These activities can be done in class, at home or in self-study time.

Suggested examples:

2.1 *Identify ideas and evidence from different perspectives within different sources, on a given topic.* Ideas from global, national, personal perspectives. Example of a national perspective: 'Globalisation has made our cities in this country more vibrant with different nationalities'

2.2 *Explain how graphical or numerical data supports an argument.* This learning objective is not a focus of lessons 4–6, so learners might still be shading in the grade they used in self-assessment 1.

2.3 *Explain causes of a local or global issue and the consequences on others.* Analysis is to break something down, for example, into causes and consequences. Analysis is more than describe, it is explaining something. For example, 'Globalisation means people are more interconnected around the world' (consequence); 'More opportunities for education for all have been created by technology' (cause: technology; consequence; more education for all opportunities). This learning objective is not a focus of lessons 4–6 so learners might still be shading in the grade they used in self-assessment 1.

2.4 *Suggest and justify different actions to make a positive difference to a national or global issue.* Basic problem-solving steps are:

- Identify the problem/issue (What is the problem? It is important that learners understand that it is something that has a course of action to help resolve it)
- Explain the issue/problem (For whom is it a problem? Why is it a problem?)
- Search for and organise information (What information do I need? Where do I get this information? Primary and/or secondary research sources?)
- Check resources needed (Is my course of action realistic? What do I need to implement it?)
- Form a plan (Who does what and when?)
- Evaluate course of action/solution (Does my solution/ course of action help resolve the issue/problem?).

Approach problem-solving by identifying the issue (as questions) and coming up with two or three possible solutions. Give reasons for and against these solutions to decide on the best and most realistic solution.

Getting better at analysis skills: Lesson 7

Lesson 7 focuses on using information from different perspectives to address an issue. It forms a sequence of learning with Lessons 8 and 9.

CAMBRIDGE STAGE 7 ANALYSIS LEARNING OBJECTIVES

2.1 Identify ideas and evidence from different perspectives within different sources on a given topic

LEARNING GOALS

To get better at:

- recognising that different perspectives on a topic/issue exist
- identifying different groups of stakeholders according to the topic/issue

How will I know if I reach my goals?

Good for: Learners to give examples of their learning from the lesson. They can complete the table at any point in the lesson, but they might do it at the end.

Resources needed

Learner's Skills Book 7; your own Language Support handout (if appropriate); quick quiz questions for the Prior learning activity (see below); Challenge topic (e.g. 'Globalisation'); Worked Example for the Main activity (below).

Prior learning (approx. 5–10 mins)

Good for: Building on previous knowledge, learning and understanding. This might be from Primary Global Perspectives, from other subject areas, or from previous Stage 7 Global Perspectives lessons (especially Section 2 'Analysis').

Activity: Review learning from Section 2 'Analysis'. Read out the quick quiz questions (see below) and learners write down answers.

Differentiation: Allow learners to look back in their Learner's Skills Book 7. Some will not need to. Learners to work individually and then share ideas with a partner/whole class in the Starter activity.

Quick quiz questions and suggested answers: Answers to be discussed in the Starter activity (see table below).

1 What is an issue?	Problem, something that needs resolving.
2 Give an example of an issue.	Loss of language/culture; poverty, etc.
3 What is an opinion/ viewpoint?	What someone thinks about something, which may / may not be supported by evidence.
4 What is a perspective?	A view of the world made up of opinions and viewpoints, supported by evidence.
5 Give an example of a perspective.	Global, national/local, personal, cultural, positive, negative.
6 What's the difference between a global and national perspective?	A global perspective may come from a specific country, organisation, institution or even an individual, but it will have influence that spreads beyond any one country. For example: 'Globalisation has more benefits than disadvantages globally.' A national perspective is based on the needs of a whole country. For example, 'Without globalisation, we would not be as economically developed as we now are and more people would be living in poverty.'
7 Give some words that signal 'causes'	because, due to, since, as, so long as … , as long as … , now that.
8 Give some words that signal 'consequences'	as a result, therefore, that's why, so, consequently, this means, this leads to, for this reason, due to this, if … then.
9 Why might a graph be useful?	To gain evidence for a perspective; to present findings from primary research.
10 What's the first step for finding a solution to an issue/problem?	Identifying the issue (as a question).

Starter activity (approx. 10 mins)

Good for: Reviewing quiz answers and learning from Section 2 'Analysis' so far.

Activity: Elicit and discuss answers to the questions in the Prior learning activity. Whole-class discussion to clarify thinking and gain new learning. Check that all learners know the answers to all outstanding questions. You might ask learners to write down questions and answers for future reference.

Suggested answers/ideas: See Prior learning activity.

Not topic specific.

Main activity (approx. 20–25 mins)

Good for: Identifying the stakeholders interested in a topic/issue, and exploring different perspectives on the topic/issue.

Activity: Give learners the issue (see Worked Example for the Main activity). Learners complete the diagram for the issue.

Differentiation: Talk through the Worked Example, eliciting/explaining why it might be important to consider different perspectives. When completing their own diagrams, learners can work in small groups for support and feedback.

Ways of working: Whole class and small groups. Whole-class discussion about stakeholders and sub-groups within these stakeholder groups.

Different opinions/perspectives: This lesson focuses on different stakeholder groups and their different perspectives on a topic/issue and also the differing perspectives within these groups.

Learner response and feedback: Encourage learners to ask each other questions such as:

- Who would be interested in this topic/issue?
- Why would they be interested?
- What might their perspective be and why?

Suggested ideas: (See Worked Example for the Main activity).

Worked Example for the Main activity

Challenge topic: Globalisation

Issue: Loss of the local language due to globalisation

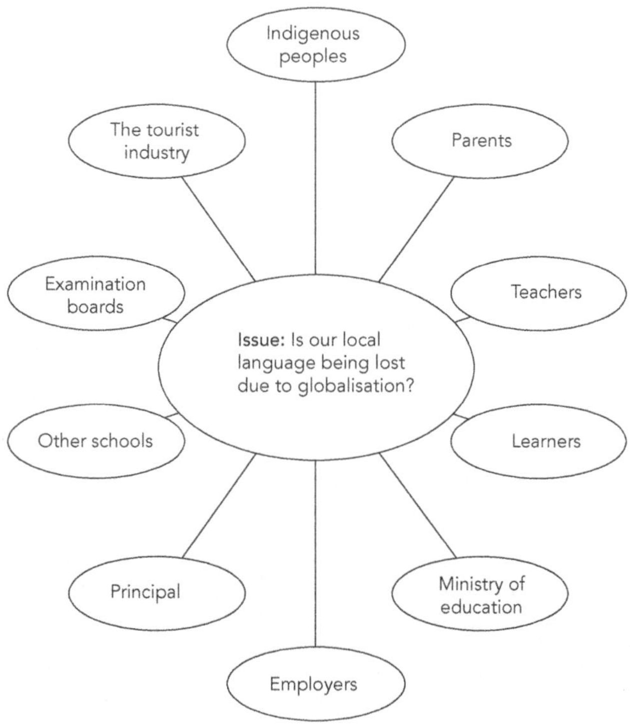

Stress that each circle contains a stakeholder group (and therefore a relevant perspective) that could inform learners' understanding of a particular issue. You can also suggest that there are sub-groups within these groups that might have differing perspectives. For example: Students – different grades might have different perspectives; Employers – the tourist industry might have a different perspective to other employers, and so on.

Suggested issues on globalisation:

Should unhealthy fast food be banned from the school canteen?

Should the meals served in the canteen be meat-free at least one day per week?

Should there be a week of cultural activities in school during the Summer term?

Should the local language be taught for an hour a week to all learners?

Should technology be used in lessons to connect with learners from other parts of the world?

Independent reflection activity (approx. 5–10 mins)

Good for: Encouraging learners to consider their learning from the lesson, what they think they have done well in terms of working on their own, joining in discussions, asking for help/support, helping their partner, and so on. Encourage learners to reflect on other skills as well as analysis skills (research, evaluation, reflection, communication, collaboration) they have used this lesson. This activity can be done in class, at home or in self-study time.

Getting better at analysis skills: Lesson 8

Lesson 8 continues the sequence from Lesson 7 and focuses on finding different perspectives in sources of information to gain information to help address an issue.

CAMBRIDGE STAGE 7 ANALYSIS LEARNING OBJECTIVES

2.1 Identify ideas and evidence from different perspectives within different sources on a given topic

2.2 Explain how graphical or numerical data supports an argument

LEARNING GOALS

To get better at:

- identifying different groups of stakeholders according to the topic/issue
- planning and carrying out steps to find another perspective
- designing a questionnaire to gain information from a different perspective to help understand a topic/issue

How will I know if I reach my goals?

Good for: Learners to give examples of their learning from the lesson. They can complete the table at any point in the lesson, but they might do it at the end.

Resources needed

Learner's Skills Book 7; your own Language Support handout (if appropriate); an issue for the Prior learning activity (see below); text (see Worked Example for the Starter activity); Challenge topic (e.g. 'Globalisation') and issue (see Worked Example for the Main activity).

Prior learning (approx. 5 mins)

Good for: Building on previous knowledge, learning and understanding. This might be from Primary Global Perspectives, from other subject areas, or from previous stage 7 Global Perspectives lessons (especially Lesson 7).

Activity: Review learning about stakeholders from Lesson 7. Give learners an issue for task 2 (e.g. Whether to ban school uniform/homework).

Differentiation: Learners can work together. Some learners will need to refer back to Lesson 7.

Suggested answers:

1. Person, group or organisation that has a direct or indirect concern or interest in something – a topic/issue
2. For example, for 'whether to ban school uniform/homework': learners, parents, teachers
3. No. Learners might like the idea of free choice of clothing, but parents might find it easier to have a uniform and not have to think about what their children wear to school.

Not topic specific.

Starter activity (approx. 10 mins)

Good for: Finding different perspectives on a topic/issue.

Activity: Give learners a short text (see Worked Example). Learners read the text and identify the perspective put forward in it.

Ways of working: Individually, in pairs and whole-class discussion to clarify thinking and gain new learning.

Suggested answers/ideas: See Worked Example.

Worked Example for the Starter activity

Challenge topic: Globalisation

TEXT: SHOULD UNHEALTHY FAST FOOD BE BANNED FROM THE SCHOOL CANTEEN?

Whilst the school canteen has always been very popular, recently parents and teachers have become concerned that learners are eating too much meat and too many fried foods, which are unhealthy. Many learners choose fried foods such as burgers and chips and often have a sugary pudding rather than fruit, which is better for them.

Now your school will decide whether to ban unhealthy fast foods.

Suggested answers:

1 Local perspective: parents and teachers at the school.

2 Learners, catering staff who make and serve the meals, suppliers (meat, fruit and veg) where the food is sourced from, and so on.

3 They have different interests so, for example, learners are likely to think differently to parents and teachers, and suppliers of meat will think differently to suppliers of vegetables and fruit.

4 Most likely by asking them in an interview, survey or questionnaire.

Main activity (approx. 20–25 mins)

Good for: Finding out information from a specific stakeholder group by designing a simple 'Yes/No' questionnaire. For this activity, the stakeholder group is other Stage 7 learners.

Activity: Learners design ten questions to find out information from a student perspective about an issue you give them. You might give each small group a different issue or they can all work on the same issue (see Worked Example). It's a good idea if learners work in teams for this activity and produce one questionnaire for completion as they will be working in these teams in Lesson 9.

Differentiation: Learners work in small groups to share ideas, give and gain feedback.

Ways of working: In teams/small groups.

Different opinions/perspectives: The lesson focuses on gaining a different perspective.

Learner response and feedback: Encourage learners to work in small groups to give feedback to each other on the questions and choose the best ten questions keeping their issue in mind. Questions to ask when compiling the questionnaire:

- Is it clear what the question is asking?
- Is the question short and to the point?
- Is the question direct (does it use 'you')?
- Can the question be answered with 'Yes/No'?
- Does the question give further information to help answer the issue question?

Learners should also ask you for feedback on their final questionnaire and then make any changes to the questions before they hand it out for completion.

Suggested answers/ideas: See Worked Example for the Main activity.

Worked Example for the Main activity

Challenge topic: Globalisation

Suggested issues:

- Should unhealthy fast food be banned from the school canteen?
- Should the meals served in the canteen be meat-free at least one day per week?
- Should there be a week of cultural activities in school during the Summer term?
- Should the local language be taught for an hour a week to all students?
- Should technology be used in lessons to connect with students from other parts of the world?

Suggested questionnaire for the issue: Should unhealthy fast food be banned from the school canteen?

Student Questionnaire – Stage 7					
Name:					
Gender:		Male		Female	
		Yes	No	Yes	No
1	Do you eat meat?				
2	Do the meals served in the canteen contain vegetables?				
3	Would you like to see more meat-free options?				
4	Should meals be meat-free at least one day per week?				
5	Is fresh fruit available every day?				
6	Does the canteen offer fried food every day?				
7	Should fried food be banned from the canteen?				
8	Do you think more fresh fish should be served in the canteen?				
9	Would you like to see more choice of salads?				
10	Would you like to see healthier food in the canteen?				

Independent reflection activity (approx. 5 mins)

Good for: Encouraging learners to consider their learning from the lesson, what they found easy and what they needed help with. Encourage learners to reflect on other skills as well as analysis skills (research, evaluation, reflection, communication, collaboration) they have used this lesson. This activity can be done in class, at home or in self-study time.

Getting better at analysis skills: Lesson 9

Lesson 9 focuses on using research already done, including the findings from the questionnaire in Lesson 8 to suggest a course of action to help resolve an issue.

CAMBRIDGE STAGE 7 ANALYSIS LEARNING OBJECTIVES

2.1 Identify ideas and evidence from different perspectives within different sources on a given topic

2.3 Explain causes of a local or global issue and consequences on others

2.4 Suggest and justify different actions to make a positive difference to a national or global issue

LEARNING GOALS

To get better at:

- gaining information from different perspectives within different sources
- explaining causes of a local issue and the consequences on others
- suggesting an action to make a positive difference to a local issue

How will I know if I reach my goals?

Good for: Learners to give examples of their learning from the lesson. They can complete the table at any point in the lesson, but they might do it at the end.

Resources needed

Learner's Skills Book 7; subject-specific words and phrases; research findings from questionnaires in Lesson 8 for Prior learning activity; Challenge topic (e.g. 'Globalisation'); Worked Example for the Starter activity; website addresses and access to the internet for the Main activity.

Prior learning (approx. 5–10 mins)

Good for: Building on previous knowledge, learning and understanding. This might be from Primary Global Perspectives, from other subject areas, or from previous Stage 7 Global Perspectives lessons. This lesson consolidates learning from the whole of Section 2.

Activity: Discuss findings from the Lesson 8 questionnaire.

Differentiation: Learners work in teams for this activity. They share their findings from the questionnaire and ask each other the questions in the Learner's Skills Book 7.

Suggested ideas: Not topic specific, but should be linked to the topic of Section 2 'Analysis', especially the questionnaire in Lesson 8.

Starter activity (approx. 10 mins)

Good for: Planning to propose a course of action to address an issue after research.

Activity: Teams work together to review the issue that was the basis of their questionnaire in Lesson 8:

- They discuss the causes of the issue and the consequences on others. For example, due to globalisation, unhealthy fast food has become widely available and it's cheaper than some healthier alternatives so has led to an increase in unhealthy fast-food meals in school. The consequences are becoming overweight, unhealthy learners, time off school due to illness, and so on.
- They discuss whether further research is needed for them to be able to suggest a course of action to help resolve the issue (too much unhealthy fast food in the school canteen).
- They discuss and suggest a course of action. They can produce the required outcome in the Main activity. For example, a letter/email, presentation, event, video clip, podcast, leaflet, and so on.

Suggested answers: Should be specific to the questionnaire issue (see Worked Example for the Starter activity).

Worked Example for the Starter activity

Challenge topic: Globalisation

Suggested issues from Lesson 8:

- Should unhealthy fast food be banned from the school canteen?
- Should the meals served in the canteen be meat-free at least one day per week?
- Should there be a week of cultural activities in school during the Summer term?
- Should the local language be taught for an hour a week to all students?
- Should technology be used in lessons to connect with students from other parts of the world?

Suggested answers:

1. Should unhealthy fast food be banned from the school canteen?
2. Conclusion is that yes, fast food should be banned, from a local perspective.
3. Yes, to gain national and global perspectives.
4. A letter to the Head Teacher to suggest a ban on fried foods such as burgers and chips and one meat-free day in the school canteen.

Main activity (approx. 20–25 mins)

Good for: Suggesting and carrying out a course of action to help resolve a local issue.

Activity: Learners work in teams. They do further research if necessary and decide who finds out what. They discuss their course of action and what they are going to produce.

Differentiation: Learners work in groups of four for feedback, support and guidance. Give some website addresses (see ideas on next page) or enable learners to look for their own.

Ways of working: Small groups to develop teamworking skills.

Different opinions/perspectives: Stress that the aim is to suggest a course of action that takes different perspectives about their issue into consideration.

Learner response and feedback: Encourage learners to give feedback to each other on the information gained. Ask questions: What else did you learn? How can we use what you've learned? Do your findings make our case for this course of action? Refer learners back to Lesson 4 about problem-solving.

Suggested ideas for Worked Example for the Starter activity:

National perspective:

- Australia: https://www.dailytelegraph.com.au/rendezview/its-time-to-ban-junk-food-for-kids-before-its-too-late/news-story/8a11094c745a680c6a43de9243cb2261

Global perspectives:

- Mexico: https://www.theguardian.com/world/2010/may/27/mexico-bans-junk-food-schools
- UK: https://www.theguardian.com/education/2004/sep/06/schools.uk1
- USA: https://well.blogs.nytimes.com/2012/05/08/bans-on-school-junk-food-pay-off-in-california

Independent reflection activity; Self-assessment; Challenge topic review (approx. 15–20 mins)

Good for: Encouraging learners to consider their learning and progression in learning in lessons. Ask them to be as honest as they can. Encourage learners to reflect on other skills as well as analysis skills (research, evaluation, reflection, communication, collaboration) they have used this lesson, for example, collaboration skills as they worked in teams.

Learners also complete the self-assessment to set their own learning targets. Learners think about and shade where they think they are at this time in their learning. 'With help' refers to guidance given (pointing a learner in the right direction, although examples should still come from the learner), for example, from you, other learners, previous work done by the learner in the Learner's Skills Book 7. For the Challenge topic review, learners explore the topic used in this section to develop analysis skills. These activities can be done in class, at home or in self-study time.

Suggested examples:

2.1 *Identify ideas and evidence from different perspectives within different sources, on a given topic.* Ideas should include global, national and local perspectives – for example 'Children within the community are getting fatter due to eating too much unhealthy fast food' (local perspective). Stakeholders might include parents, teachers, Head Teacher, medical profession and health agencies.

2.2 *Explain how graphical or numerical data supports an argument.* A graph is one way of presenting research findings. Learners might write that they need support / can help others with labelling the axis or doing a double-bar graph for the comparison of data (e.g., between boys and girls).

2.3 *Explain causes of a local or global issue and the consequences on others.* For example:

- Words/phrases that signal causes – because, due to, since, as, so long as … , as long as … , now that
- Words/phrases that signal consequences – as a result, therefore, that's why, so, consequently, this means, this leads to, for this reason, due to this, if … then.

2.4 *Suggest and justify different actions to make a positive difference to a national or global issue.* Relevant courses of action for a specific local issue might include giving a talk or presentation to raise awareness that the issue needs everyone to participate for it to be resolved; posters or leaflets to promote the importance of something to help resolve a local issue; an event where people actively do something to help resolve an issue.

Section 3 Evaluation

Introduction

The learning objectives and learning goals for evaluation skills for Stage 7 focus on the following:

- Evaluating sources
- Evaluating arguments

However, you might also find opportunities within the lessons to develop some of the other Global Perspectives skills. For example, when selecting, organising and recording relevant information from a range of sources and findings from research, using appropriate methods, not only will learners be developing evaluation skills, they will also be developing their research skills.

The ideas given in this Teacher's Book 7 are suggestions only, and the activities can be used with any of the Global Perspectives Challenge topics for Stages 7 to 9, although Worked Examples are provided for some learning activities. It is hoped that the ideas in this Teacher's Book 7 will help you structure your lessons in an active learning way with input from you as the teacher to help guide and support learners to become more effective at being able to evaluate sources and arguments when exploring information to answer research questions.

Evaluation skills overview

Learning objectives	3.1 Evaluate sources, considering the author and purpose, recognising that some sources may be biased 3.2 Discuss the effectiveness of a source, making explicit reference to its development of an argument
Challenge topic ideas	Digital world; Employment; Humans and other species
Key points	• Understanding the difference between analysis and evaluation • Knowing how to recognise 'fake' news • There are different ways that a source can be unreliable, for example, being out of date • There are two definitions for an argument • Knowing the difference between fact and opinion • Understanding what bias is • Appreciating that most sources of information contain some form of bias • Understanding the difference between numerical evidence and narrative evidence • Saying what it means to test a claim
Language support	• Pre-teach key vocabulary: evaluation; strengths; April fool jokes; reliable, unreliable, fake news, news links, author, social media; evidence; claim; conclusion; premise; logical; reason; believable; debate; fact; opinion; bias; numerical evidence; narrative evidence. Also include any topic-specific vocabulary for the Challenge topics – Digital world; Employment; Humans and other species.

Cross-skills links	
	1 **Research**
	1.2 Identify and begin to reference a range of print and multimedia sources and use them to locate relevant information and answer research questions.
	1.3 Select an appropriate method and conduct research to test predictions and begin to answer a research question.
	1.4 Select, organise and record relevant information from a range of sources and findings from research, using appropriate methods.
	2 **Analysis**
	2.1 Identify ideas and evidence from different perspectives within different sources on a given topic.
	2.2 Explain how graphical or numerical data supports an argument.
	4 **Reflection**
	4.3 Consider ways that personal perspective on an issue may have changed as a result of conducting research or exploring different perspectives.
	4.4 Identify skills learned or improved during an activity and relate to personal strengths and areas for improvement.
	5 **Collaboration**
	5.1 The team assign roles and divide tasks fairly, considering the skills of team members and time available, and work together to achieve a shared outcome.
	5.2 The team member introduces useful ideas to help achieve a shared outcome and works positively to resolve conflict, solve problems and encourage other team members to participate, when required.
	6 **Communication**
	6.1 Present information and arguments clearly with some reasoning, referencing sources where appropriate.
	6.2 Listen to ideas and information and offer relevant and well-judged contributions that demonstrate understanding of the issue.

Starting with evaluation skills: Lesson 1

Lesson 1 focuses on identifying what the term 'evaluation' means and the difference between evaluation and analysis.

CAMBRIDGE STAGE 7 EVALUATION LEARNING OBJECTIVES

3.1 Evaluate sources, considering the author and purpose, recognising that some sources may be biased

LEARNING GOALS

To start to:

- understand what the term 'evaluation' means
- understand the difference between evaluation and analysis
- recognise that some news might be 'fake' news

How will I know if I reach my goals?

Good for: Learners to give examples of their learning from the lesson. They can complete the table at any point in the lesson, but they might do it at the end.

Resources needed

Learner's Skills Book 7; your own Language Support handout (if appropriate); Challenge topic, e.g. Digital world; fake news stories/websites (can be topic related) and internet access (see Worked Example for the Main activity below).

Prior learning (approx. 5 mins)

Good for: Building on previous knowledge, learning and understanding. This might be from Primary Global Perspective, from other subjects or from previous Stage 7 Global Perspectives lessons.

Activity: Introduction to the term 'evaluation'.

Differentiation: Learners might not be able to come up with reasons. Learners work in pairs to discuss and then write own ideas. Class discussion about answers to questions but more importantly leading into discussion about what the term 'evaluation' means.

Suggested answers:

1 a and **b**: We discuss issues that are in the news, which are relevant to me and my family/friends; allows us to share our opinion; not just learning about specific topic but developing skills for all subjects and that will be useful in life.

1 c and **d**: I'm unable to work on my own enough as there is a lot of pair and group work; I'm not confident enough to share my opinion; I prefer to work with my friends rather in the groups the teacher assigns me to.

2 Analysis is explaining something in more detail such as reasons for/against something/causes/ consequences, and so on.

Evaluation is strengths/weaknesses of something with reasons; making a judgement about something (quality, importance, value, etc.).

Not topic specific.

Starter activity (approx. 10 mins)

Good for: Exploring the difference between evaluation and analysis.

Activity: Learners decide whether the statements are evaluation or analysis.

Ways of working: Individually, in pairs and whole-class discussion.

Suggested answers:

1 Evaluation: **A**, **B**, **E**; Analysis **C**, **D**, **F**.

Remind learners of the words that signal causes and consequences for analysis from Section 2. Evaluation is a judgement about something.

2 Their own statements to check understanding.

Not topic specific.

Main activity (approx. 20–25 mins)

Good for: Enabling learners to start thinking about the amount of time they spend looking for information and whether this information can be trusted or not.

Activity: Give learners news stories or relevant website addresses – some that are real items and some that are fake. Learners answer the questions individually and then take part in class discussion about the answers (see Worked Example for the Main activity).

Differentiation: Class discussion. Choice of 'fake' news stories/websites. Learners can work in pairs.

Ways of working: Individually, in pairs, whole-class discussion.

Different opinions/perspectives: Also encourage learners to look at the fake news stories from different perspectives, i.e. who might think these stories are true and why?

Learner response and feedback: Encourage learners to discuss with each other for **F**. Questions to ask:

- What is the news story about?
- Does it make sense to you?
- Does it seem like a joke to you?
- Do you think this is possible? Why? Why not?

Suggested answers/ideas: See Worked Example for the Main activity.

Worked Example for the Main activity

Challenge topic: Digital world

Suggested answers:

1
- **a** Answers will vary
- **b** Online news, TV news, radio/podcast news, newspapers/magazines, social media, books, ask teacher/parents/friends
- **c** Teacher because they are knowledgeable about the subject and want me to do well. Parents as they want me to learn things
- **d** A printed, broadcast or digital report of factual information about important events in the world, country or local area
- **e** News presented as fact but actually made up
- **f** Answers will depend on the website addresses given. The following are based on the Challenge topic 'Digital world' and are all fake
  1. https://www.youtube.com/watch?time_continue=2&v=RkJZDvHMyTA Japanese keyboard
  2. https://www.youtube.com/watch?time_continue=29&v=QAwL0O5nXe0 Google cloud
  3. https://blog.google/products/chromebooks/all-best-mobile-accessories-now-your-chromebook Chromebook (Update on the website says they aren't real)

     All of Google's 'April fool' jokes can be found here: https://www.theverge.com/2017/3/31/15140206/google-best-april-fools-jokes-roundup-2017
- **g** Answers will vary and be limited at this stage: seems like a joke; the date isn't correct, for example SMART phones weren't invented until 1992; too good to be true; seems ridiculous; check web address, e.g. abcnews.com.co is fake as is abcnews.org.uk; check author, use a fact checker (factcheck.org; snopes.com; The Washington post fact checker).

Independent reflection activity (approx. 5–10 mins)

Good for: Learners to give examples of what they have found the most difficult in the lesson. This might be skill or content specific, for example, judging whether news stories are real or fake. Encourage learners to reflect on other skills as well as evaluation skills (research, analysis, reflection, communication, collaboration) they have used this lesson. This activity can be done in class, at home or in self-study time.

Starting with evaluation skills: Lesson 2

Lesson 2 focuses on recognising fake sources of information and follows on from Lesson 1.

CAMBRIDGE STAGE 7 EVALUATION LEARNING OBJECTIVES

3.1 Evaluate sources, considering the author and purpose, recognising that some sources may be biased

LEARNING GOALS

To start to:

- recognise whether an information source is real or fake
- understand how to evaluate an information source

How will I know if I reach my goals?

Good for: Learners to give examples of their learning from the lesson. They can complete the table at any point in the lesson, but they might do it at the end.

Resources needed

Learner's Skills Book 7; your own Language Support handout (if appropriate); Challenge topic (e.g. Human and other species) and related fake news website address for the Starter activity; Worked Example for the Main activity.

Prior learning (approx. 5 mins)

Good for: Building on previous knowledge, learning and understanding. This might be from Primary Global Perspectives, from other subject areas, and from their last Global Perspectives lesson.

Activity: Ask learners to answer the questions in their Learner's Skills Book 7.

Differentiation: Learners work individually or in pairs. Learners can look back at Lesson 1 if they need to.

Suggested answers:

1 a A printed, broadcast or digital report of factual information about important events in the world, country or local area

b News or stories on the internet that are not true / made up

c A fake / made up website such as http://abcnews.com.co

d Make money, to mislead people, to influence people, for political gain, and so on

e Stories spread quickly, as they are shared via social media and can reach many more people. The source of the information gets lost.

Not topic specific.

Starter activity (approx. 5 mins)

Good for: Starting to look at information sources to judge whether they are real or fake (reliable or unreliable).

Activity: Initial look at the website and form some judgement with some reasoning. See Worked Example for the Main activity below.

Ways of working: Individually, in pairs and whole-class discussion to explore whether the source is real or fake – initial thoughts.

Suggested ideas: Fake news website address for the Challenge topic 'Humans and other species': http://zapatopi.Net/treeoctopus (Tree octopus).

Main activity (approx. 20–25 mins)

Good for: Further exploration of whether an information source is real or fake and how to tell, continuing from the Starter activity.

Activity: Learners complete the checklist and then answer the question from the Starter activity again, but with new knowledge and understanding of how to tell whether an information source is real or fake. See Worked Example.

Differentiation: Can work in pairs. Don't need to complete the whole table. Can add notes as appropriate but there might not be any.

Ways of working: Individually, in pairs or whole class to share ideas, clarify own thinking/understanding.

Different opinions/perspectives: Encourage learners to see why some might believe this story.

Learner response and feedback: Learners ask each other why they have noted what they have. Encourage learners to explore the website together with the checklist and to click on the links asking each other if they believe what they are reading.

Suggested answers: These will vary according to the website address given. See Worked Example.

Worked Example for the Main activity

Challenge topic: Humans and other species

Article discussing the made up Tree octopus website: https://www.dailymail.co.uk/news/article-1352929/Endangered-tree-octopus-proves-students-believe-read-internet.html

Suggested answers:

1

	Yes/ No	Notes
1	Yes	But only as fake
2	No	
3	No	
4	No	
5	No	Name of person that made up the story – Lyle Zapato
6	No	
7	Yes	'Write your representatives' missing 'to'
8	Yes	He has a book on Amazon
9	No	He adds blogs regularly even though the tree octopus is made up
10	No	Links do not support the existence of a tree octopus

3 a So that we don't believe everything we read and we question things and look for further evidence to support any claims made

b For people to make money, to mislead people, to make them think that something is real when it is not

c Learners use the checklist given in the Learner's Skills Book 7

d Are they too good to be true? Answers will vary.

Independent reflection activity (approx. 5–10 mins)

Good for: Encouraging learners to consider what they found difficult during the lesson. Ask them to be as honest as they can. There is no correct response and they can choose more than one. Encourage explanation but not all learners will be able to do this. Encourage learners to reflect on other skills as well as evaluation skills (research, analysis, reflection, communication, collaboration) they have used this lesson. This activity can be done in class, at home or in self-study time.

Starting with evaluation skills: Lesson 3

Lesson 3 focuses on further understanding of judging whether a source is reliable to use or not and follows on from Lessons 1 and 2.

CAMBRIDGE STAGE 7 EVALUATION LEARNING OBJECTIVES

3.1 Evaluate sources, considering the author and purpose, recognising that some sources may be biased

LEARNING GOALS

To start to:

- understand how to tell when an information source is 'fake'
- identify reliable sources of information
- identify some information from a source for a specific purpose

How will I know if I reach my goals?

Good for: Learners to give examples of their learning from the lesson. They can complete the table at any point in the lesson, but they might do it at the end.

Resources needed

Learner's Skills Book 7; your own Language Support handout (if appropriate); Challenge topic (e.g. Digital world), reliable information source (see Worked Example for the Starter activity); internet access.

Prior learning (approx. 5 mins)

Good for: Building on previous knowledge, learning and understanding. This might be from Primary Global Perspectives, from other subject areas, or from previous Global Perspectives lessons.

Activity: Learners write down three ways of telling whether a source is fake. Share with partner and class. To review learning and create discussion.

Differentiation: Learners work in pairs. Can look back at work done previously (Lesson 2). Discuss responses in class.

Suggested answers: Any reasonable and relevant response. For example, check the date; check the author; is the story believable / a joke? check other stories about the same issue; check the website address, and so on.

Not topic specific.

Starter activity (approx. 10–15 mins)

Good for: Exploring a reliable source of information using the checklist.

Activity: Give learners a website address that you (and perhaps they) know is real/reliable and ask them to complete the table to judge/check whether it's real or fake. Generate discussion about the checklist.

Differentiation: Add notes to table, work in pairs.

Suggested answers/ideas: See Worked Example.

Worked Example for the Starter activity

Challenge topic: Digital world; any topic can be used, but better if the same topic as the Main activity.

Information source: Video clip from the BBC about addiction to gaming.

https://www.bbc.co.uk/news/av/uk-34231719/more-teenagers-addicted-to-computer-games. This reliable/real source of information is a bit out of date (2015), uses real people, is from the BBC, which is known to be a reputable source of information.

	Checklist	Source	Notes
1	Has the story been reported anywhere else?	Yes	A few different websites report on this issue, including *The Guardian*.
2	Is it on the radio, TV or in the newspapers?	TV and Online	
3	Have you heard of the organisation that published the story?	Yes	BBC is known as a reputable organisation for news.
4	Does the website where you found the story look real?	Yes	
5	Does the website address at the very top of the page look real?	Yes	
6	Does the story sound believable?	Yes	
7	Are there any errors in spelling or grammar?	No	
8	Is the author a real person?	Yes	
9	Is there anything odd about the dates?	2015	A bit old.
10	Is there any other evidence to support the story?	Yes	Testimony from mother and child.

Main activity (approx. 20–25 mins)

Good for: Finding relevant information sources for a specific purpose (research question given by you).

Activity: Give learners a research question, for example: 'Do you think scientists should continue to develop robots?'

1 Learners search for three websites where they might find reliable information to do with the topic/help them answer the question.

2 Learners complete the checklist table to help them judge whether each information source is reliable or not.

3 Learners decide with new knowledge from their completed table whether or not to use the information sources originally chosen.

4 Learners should check the question and only include details in the blog that relate to the question. They note the key points in their own words; keep it relatively short (no more than 100 words) and include linking words as necessary (because, due to, this means, etc.)

Differentiation: Learners can work individually and share in pairs once complete or work in pairs and share in fours.

Ways of working: Individually or in pairs for support and to clarify own thinking and understanding.

Different opinions/perspectives: Learners should keep in mind that the ideas in their sources might come from different perspectives, which is fine as long as the sources can be judged as reliable.

Learner response and feedback: Learners can help each other using the checklist, asking questions such as:

- Have you read the whole story and not just the headline?
- Have you checked the author exists?
- Have you checked the date of the story?
- Does the story seem believable or a joke?
- Does the source refer to any other evidence – real people, other sources of information?

Peer feedback about blogs to determine whether the information gained from the sources actually starts to help answer the research question given.

Suggested answers: Answers will vary as different learners will use different websites / sources of information. Learners can explore how and why blogs are different in relation to the other information sources used.

Independent reflection activity; Self-assessment; Challenge topic review (approx. 15–20 mins)

Good for: Encouraging learners to consider their learning in lessons. Encourage learners to reflect on other skills as well as evaluation skills (research, analysis, reflection, communication, collaboration) they have used this lesson, for example, research skills as they selected which websites to use.

Learners also complete the self-assessment to set their own learning targets before they move on. Learners think about and shade where they think they are at this time in their learning. 'With help' refers to guidance given (pointing a learner in the right direction, although examples should still come from the learner), for example, from you, other learners, previous work done by the learner in the Learner's Skills Book 7. For the Challenge topic review, learners explore the topic used in this section to develop evaluation skills. These activities can be done in class, at home or in self-study time.

Suggested examples:

3.1 *Evaluate sources, considering the author and purpose, recognising that some sources may be biased.* Using the criteria in the checklist; checking the author exists and looking at the purpose of the information source to see if it's real or not. Bias has not been a focus of Lessons 1–3, but will be explored more in Lesson 7.

3.2 *Discuss the effectiveness of a source, making explicit reference to its development of an argument.* This learning objective is not covered in Lessons 1–3, but is covered in Lesson 4–6.

Developing evaluation skills: Lesson 4

Lesson 4 focuses on understanding what an argument is in Global Perspectives. It follows on from work done to evaluate an information source in Lessons 1–3.

CAMBRIDGE STAGE 7 EVALUATION LEARNING OBJECTIVES

3.2 Discuss the effectiveness of a source, making explicit reference to its development of an argument

LEARNING GOALS

To develop knowledge and understanding about:

- what an 'argument' is
- what makes an effective argument

How will I know if I reach my goals?

Good for: Learners to give examples of their learning from the lesson. They can complete the table at any point in the lesson, but they might do it at the end.

Resources needed

Learner's Skills Book 7; your own Language Support handout (if appropriate); Challenge topic (e.g. 'Employment') and video clip for the Starter activity (see below); Challenge topic (e.g. 'Employment') and text (see Worked Example for the Main activity).

Prior learning (approx. 5–10 mins)

Good for: Building on previous knowledge, learning and understanding. This might be from Primary Global Perspectives, from other subject areas, or from previous Stage 7 Global Perspectives lessons.

Activity: Learners circle the words they think relate to an argument.

Differentiation: Allow learners to work in pairs for support, look up unknown words if not pre-taught. Ask them just to circle three or four words.

Suggested answers/ideas: There are two meanings of the word 'argument'. For Global Perspectives lessons, words that learners circle: reasoning; support for an idea; premise; claim; debate; conclusion; logical; evidence.

A useful video clip to explore what an argument is: https://www.youtube.com/watch?v=pP8dWURrEF0

Not topic specific.

Starter activity (approx. 10–15 mins)

Good for: Getting learners to think about deconstructing arguments/identifying what makes up an argument.

Activity: Learners watch a video clip related to the topic in which they will be able to identify arguments and reasons; for example, 'Why work?' https://www.youtube.com/watch?v=J8hdWy_Y9oM

Ways of working: Individually, in pairs and whole-class discussion.

Suggested answers (based on the suggested video clip): For money to buy food, clothes and gifts; for family; because they love their work; want to change the world; work for the betterment of science and humanity; work to break records like athletes; to change things, like politicians; to go higher up; for their nation; for God/religion; for fame; to make us feel good about ourselves.

Main activity (approx. 20–25 mins)

Good for: Exploring what makes up an argument.

Activity: Give learners a text (see Worked Example for the Main activity). Learners identify the claim, reasons and evidence for this claim and whether the argument is convincing and why/why not.

Differentiation: Learners can work in pairs for support. Consider the length of text (shorter or longer depending on learners) and the complexity of language (adaptations might be needed or pre-teaching vocabulary or provide your own Language Support handout).

Ways of working: Individually or in pairs to share ideas, clarify own thinking. Whole-class discussion once the argument has been evaluated.

Different opinions/perspectives: Encourage learners to consider what perspective the ideas in the text are from. For example, for the Worked Example – in favour of teaching as a career; from a social perspective, from a global perspective (evidence from three sources supporting teaching as a career).

Learner response and feedback: Encourage learners to ask questions of each other:

- What do you think the author thinks?
- Why do you think the author thinks this?
- How do you know this?

Suggested answers: Depends on the text given. See Worked Example.

Worked Example for the Main activity

Challenge topic: Employment

Suggested text:

TEACHING: A REALLY WORTHWHILE CAREER CHOICE

If you want a really worthwhile job that allows you to make a genuine and lasting difference in the world, then why not become a teacher?

You might have heard that teachers are not well paid, but money isn't everything. Quality of life is far more important, and teachers get a lot of free time. As a teacher, you can make a real difference to the lives of your students, doing something you enjoy teaching like drama, art or critical thinking skills so that your students can survive in the world without you.

According to Georgina Potter, who has taught English for 20 years at different schools around the world, 'There is nothing better than when a student tells you how much they enjoy a certain text and want to know more about it or when you see a text come to life in a drama production.'

Most people only work for money and they can't wait for the evenings, weekends and holidays, but with teaching, it doesn't have to be like that. What if you felt excited about going to your job every day, and the pay was an added bonus? As Irfan Kharti of Global School, Agra states, 'I don't think of myself as an employee at all. I know that I am a friend and a mentor to my students and colleagues. I love my job, and I get well paid to do it. I am very fortunate.'

So, are teachers generally happy? In a large study conducted in 2013, by the Centre for Job Satisfaction in Texas, of 15000 graduates who had been in the same job for more than five years, teachers reported the most sense of fulfilment in their jobs.

With teaching, you can have a fulfilling career and a family as teachers mostly work the same hours as students, so families can have time together in the evenings, at weekends and take holidays together – definitely a plus point for teaching as a career.

There are just so many reasons to become a teacher, not least you can teach something you love and get to spend more time with family and friends. Teaching is the best job in the world.

Suggested answers:

1 a Teaching is a worthwhile job to consider / best job in the world.

b Reason(s): Teach something you love; have more time to spend with family and friends; get well paid.

Evidence: Georgina Potter's statement; Irfan Kharti's statement; the study done by the Centre for Job Satisfaction, Texas.

c and **d** Answers will vary.

Independent reflection activity (approx. 5–10 mins)

Good for: Encouraging learners to consider their learning from the lesson about whether they are starting to get a better understanding of what an argument is. Encourage learners not only to write what an argument is made up of but also to give basic examples if they can (some will struggle).

For example: An argument is made up of a claim (going to university is a good idea), reason(s) (it helps you get a well-paid job) and evidence (a report showing that those who went to university earn more than those that didn't).

Encourage learners to reflect on other skills as well as evaluation skills (research, analysis, reflection, communication, collaboration) they have used this lesson. This activity can be done in class, at home or in self-study time.

Developing evaluation skills: Lesson 5

Lesson 5 focuses on the features of an argument, understanding what a claim, reason and evidence are and how to recognise them in an argument.

CAMBRIDGE STAGE 7 EVALUATION LEARNING OBJECTIVES

3.2 Discuss the effectiveness of a source, making explicit reference to its development of an argument

LEARNING GOALS

To develop knowledge and understanding about:

- how to identify a claim
- how to write a claim
- what is meant by the word 'evidence'

How will I know if I reach my goals?

Good for: Learners to give examples of their learning from the lesson. They can complete the table at any point in the lesson, but they might do it at the end.

Resources needed

Learner's Skills Book 7; your own Language Support handout (if appropriate); Challenge topic (e.g. 'Employment', but any topic suitable) for the starter and main activities; picture (see Worked Example for the Starter activity); Worked Example for the Main activity.

Prior learning (approx. 5–10 mins)

Good for: Building on previous knowledge, learning and understanding. This might be from Primary Global Perspectives, from other subject areas, or from previous Stage 7 Global Perspectives lessons.

Activity: Review learning from Lesson 4: Learners choose the correct response.

Differentiation: Allow learners to look back in their Learner's Skills Book 7. Some will not need to. Learners to work individually and then share ideas with a partner/whole class. Some learners will struggle with task 3. Class discussion to gain ideas.

Suggested answers:

1 **B**

2 **A** Why does the author think this? Reason(s)

C How does the author know this? Evidence

3 Claim: Teaching is the best career in the world; Robots create unemployment.

Reason: It's well paid and you get lots of holidays; They can do jobs that humans can do and work longer hours without needing a break.

Evidence: A report from ..... / A questionnaire about .... / ....said ....

Starter activity (approx. 10 mins)

Good for: Exploring the type of claims people can make.

Activity: Show learners a picture (see Worked Example for the Starter activity). Learners write down as many claims connected to the picture as they can in the time limit.

Ways of working: Individually, in pairs and whole-class discussion.

Suggested answers: Depends on the picture given (see Worked Example).

Not topic specific.

Worked Example for the Starter activity

Challenge topic: Employment

Picture ideas: work–life balance

- Life balance choices signpost: https://www.istockphoto.com/gb/photo/life-balance-choices-signpost-with-sunrise-sky-backgrounds-gm660654466-120460759
- Work–life word cloud: https://www.istockphoto.com/gb/photo/work-life-balance-word-cloud-on-tablet-gm658152490-120011935
- Work– life balance is an outdated myth: http://www.executivestyle.com.au/why-worklife-balance-is-an-outdated-myth-103uyx

Suggested answers:

Claims: I believe … people only work for money; family is more important than money; health is more important than money; we can't do anything without money; all work creates stress; you can't work without enough sleep, and so on.

Main activity (approx. 20–25 mins)

Good for: Gaining evidence to test a claim.

Activity: Learners write a questionnaire to test a claim about the topic (see Worked Example for the Main activity). Review how to write a questionnaire from Section 1 'Research' Lesson 5. Once complete, learners should give their questionnaire to at least ten people to complete before the next lesson when they will present their findings.

Differentiation: Learners can work in pairs for support. They can look back at Section 1 'Research' Lesson 5 to remind them how to write a questionnaire and about good and bad questions. Some learners might write fewer or less complex questions. You could give learners a good/bad example of a question for the topic or ask them to produce a bad/good question beforehand.

Ways of working: Individually or in pairs to share ideas and clarify own thinking. Whole-class discussion about questionnaires before learners start work.

Different opinions/perspectives: Learners are producing a questionnaire to gain information from a local perspective as they will give their questionnaire to family, classmates and friends to complete.

Learner response and feedback: Encourage learners to discuss in pairs / as a class the type of questions they produce. They can ask each other questions such as:

- Is the question relevant to the topic?
- Does the question allow the claim to be tested?
- Does the question need a yes/no answer?
- Does the question need an open response, and if so, how much space do we leave / how much are we expecting people to write?
- Are there too many / too few questions?
- How long will it take people to complete the survey/questionnaire?
- Are the questions clear?

Suggested answers: Stress to learners that the type of questions they ask will depend on the type of information they want to find out. They may not just be able to do this with yes/no questions, but might need more open-ended questions (see Worked Example).

Worked Example for the Main activity

Challenge topic: Employment

Example questions to test the claim 'People only work for money'

1 What type of work do you do? Employed, unemployed, unpaid work – for example, looking after children, cooking, shopping, voluntary, and so on.

2 Why do you work? For money; to interact with others; to make a difference; to have a more fulfilling life, and so on.

3 Did you choose the job you have? Why?

4 What are the benefits of having your job?

5 What are the disadvantages of having your job?

6 What does your job enable you to do? (buy things, pay bills, go on holiday, etc.)

7 What can't you do because you have a job? (travel for a month; spend enough time with family and friends, do voluntary work, etc.)
8 Does your job give you a sense of fulfilment/purpose/satisfaction?
9 What is more important to you: money or job satisfaction?
10 Do you think people only work for money? Why? Why not?

Independent reflection activity (approx. 5–10 mins)

Good for: Encouraging learners to reflect on their own learning from the lesson and ways that they might have helped others. Encourage learners to reflect on other skills as well as evaluation skills (research, analysis, reflection, communication, collaboration) they have used this lesson. This activity can be done in class, at home or in self-study time.

Developing evaluation skills: Lesson 6

Lesson 6 focuses on producing information from a questionnaire to help test a claim.

CAMBRIDGE STAGE 7 EVALUATION LEARNING OBJECTIVES

3.2 Discuss the effectiveness of a source, making explicit reference to its development of an argument

LEARNING GOALS

To develop knowledge and understanding about:

- how to test a claim
- different types of evidence
- writing relevant questions

How will I know if I reach my goals?

Good for: Learners to give examples of their learning from the lesson. They can complete the table at any point in the lesson, but they might do it at the end.

Resources needed

Learner's Skills Book 7; Your own Language Support handout (if appropriate); list of questions (see Worked Example for the Starter activity); questionnaires and responses from Lesson 5 for the Main activity.

Prior learning (approx. 5–10 mins)

Good for: Building on previous knowledge, learning and understanding. This might be from Primary Global Perspectives, from other subject areas, or from previous Stage 7 Global Perspectives lessons (Lesson 5).

Activity: Explain the difference between a structured survey (questionnaire) and an unstructured interview.

Differentiation: Allow learners to look back in their Learner's Skills Book 7. Some will not need to. Learners can work in pairs for support. Learners can revisit what they've written after class discussion to deepen their understanding.

Suggested answers: Any reasonable and relevant response. For example:

- Surveys/questionnaires are mostly used as a way of gaining numerical evidence using structured questionnaires, where most questions are 'closed' questions requiring a yes/no answer or for respondents to choose from a list (perhaps multiple choice). A survey is normally fairly short and it doesn't take long to complete. Information can be gained from a lot of people in a relatively short amount of time.
- Interviews take longer and cannot be conducted with as many people as a survey. Questions are generally more open-ended, requiring longer responses and interviewers encourage respondents to talk in more depth than they can in a survey. This type of evidence is known as narrative evidence.

Starter activity (approx. 10–15 mins)

Good for: Identifying narrative and numerical evidence.

Activity: Reviewing different types of evidence. Put some questions to do with the topic on the board (see Worked Example for the Starter activity). Learners identify the type of evidence the questions will get: numerical or narrative. Explain these two concepts to learners.

Ways of working: Individually, in pairs and whole-class discussion.

Suggested answers/ideas: See Worked Example.

Worked Example for the Starter activity

Challenge topic: Employment

Suggested questions for discussion:

1 Why do you work? **A** For money; **B** To interact with others; **C** To make a difference; **D** To have a more fulfilling life. (*Numerical evidence as a choice*)

2 Did you choose the job you have? (*Numerical as yes/no*) Why? (*Narrative – reasons*)

3 What are the benefits of having your job? (*Narrative – more than one answer unless you give a choice as in question 1*)

4 What are the disadvantages of having your job? (*As question 3*)

5 Does your job give you a sense of fulfilment/purpose/satisfaction? (*Numerical as yes/no response*)

6 What is more important to you: money or job satisfaction? (*Numerical as it stands as choice of two*)

7 Do you think people only work for money? (*Numerical for yes/no*) Why? Why not? (*Narrative for reasons*)

8 Do you like your job? (*Numerical as yes/no response*).

Main activity (approx. 20–25 mins)

Good for: Evaluating the questions asked to test a claim and presenting the information gained.

Activity: Learners look at their questions from Lesson 5 and discuss the type of answers they received. Learners present the information they gained from their questionnaire and then evaluate their questions using the questions in the Learner's Skills Book 7. They work with a partner.

Differentiation: Learners work in pairs for support. Some will find tasks 3 and 6 a challenge so might need peer support. Refer learners to the 'Tips' in their Learner's Skills Book 7 for definitions of 'relevant' and 'testing a claim'.

Ways of working: Pairs to share ideas, clarify own thinking and as support.

Different opinions/perspectives: The activity focuses on presenting information from a questionnaire to obtain a local perspective on the topic/issue.

Learner response and feedback: Encourage learners to give feedback to each other by discussing each of the questions in their questionnaire to answer the questions in the Learner's Skills Book 7.

Suggested answers: Answers will vary according to the questions asked and the information gained.

Independent reflection activity; Self-assessment; Challenge topic review (approx. 15–20 mins)

Good for: Encouraging learners to consider their and their partner's learning and progression in learning in lessons. Ask them to be as honest as they can.

Learners also complete the self-assessment to set their own learning targets before they move on. Learners think about and shade where they think they are at this time in their learning. 'With help' refers to guidance given (pointing a learner in the right direction, although examples should still come from the learner), for example, from you, other learners, previous work done by the learner in the Learner's Skills Book 7. For the Challenge topic review, learners explore the topic used in this section to develop evaluation skills. These activities can be done in class, at home or in self-study time.

Suggested examples:

3.1 *Evaluate sources, considering the author and purpose, recognising that some sources may be biased.* Using the criteria in the checklist; checking the author exists and looking at the purpose of the information source to see if it's real or not. Bias has not yet been a focus of lessons, but will be explored more in Lesson 7.

3.2 *Discuss the effectiveness of a source, making explicit reference to its development of an argument.* An argument is made up of a claim, reasoning and evidence. Being able to identify the elements of an argument: claim (what the author believes), reason(s) (why the author believes this), evidence (how the author knows this).

Getting better at evaluation skills: Lesson 7

Lesson 7 focuses on the difference between fact and opinion and identifying fact, opinion and bias in information sources.

CAMBRIDGE STAGE 7 EVALUATION LEARNING OBJECTIVES

3.1 Evaluate sources, considering the author and purpose, recognising that some sources may be biased

3.2 Discuss the effectiveness of a source, making explicit reference to its development of an argument

LEARNING GOALS

To get better at:

- knowing the difference between fact and opinion
- identifying bias when I see it

How will I know if I reach my goals?

Good for: Learners to give examples of their learning from the lesson. They can complete the table at any point in the lesson, but they might do it at the end.

Resources needed

Learner's Skills Book 7; your own Language Support handout (if appropriate); text (see Worked Example for the Starter activity); research question (see Worked Example for the Main activity), internet access.

Prior learning (approx. 5–10 mins)

Good for: Building on previous knowledge, learning and understanding. This might be from Primary Global Perspectives, from other subject areas, or from previous Stage 7 Global Perspectives lessons.

Activity: Review learning of Global Perspectives terms: fact, opinion and bias.

Differentiation: Allow learners to look at the tips box in their Learner's Skills Book 7. Some will not need to. Learners to work individually and then share ideas with a partner / whole class or can work as pairs.

Suggested ideas: Discussion about what a fact, opinion and bias are.

Starter activity (approx. 10 mins)

Good for: Identifying examples of fact, opinion and bias.

Activity: Give out a short text related to the topic (see Worked Example for the Starter activity). Learners identify a fact, opinion and bias from the text.

Suggested answers: Depend on the text given, but see Worked Example.

Not necessarily topic specific.

Worked Example for the Starter activity

Challenge topic: Digital world

Suggested text:

Technology is making our lives better. I know this because of my work in the university researching how robots can be used in the health system. Treating disease is a lot quicker and easier now that we can use new technologies to test samples in our laboratory. My colleague, Dr Evans, says that social media helps us to make friends, and so reduce loneliness, especially amongst the elderly. Results from a study done by the United Nations in 2017 show that new technology has increased economic development, creating wealth and reducing the amount of poverty.

Suggested answers: Depends on the text given. Main learning is identifying the difference between fact, opinion and bias.

Fact: Results from a study done by the United Nations in 2017 show that new technology has increased economic development, creating wealth and reducing the amount of poverty. (Comes from a cited study).

Opinion: My colleague, Dr Evans, says that social media helps us to make friends, and so reduce loneliness especially amongst the elderly. (Opinion because there is no evidence in support).

Bias: Technology is making our lives better. I know this because of my work in the university researching how robots can be used in the health system. Treating disease is a lot quicker and easier now that we can use new technologies to test samples in our laboratory. (Bias because the author is in favour of new technologies because they work in a hospital that uses them.)

Main activity (approx. 20–25 mins)

Good for: Finding relevant information related to a research question.

Activity: Suggest research questions to learners so that they can choose one (see Worked Example). Learners research to find relevant sources of information and complete the table, identifying at least one fact, opinion and example of bias.

Differentiation: Learners can work in pairs/small groups. Each member of the group can look for different features in different sources – for example, one team member looks for facts, another for opinions, and so on. Learners should write down the examples they find. They can find more than one of each.

Ways of working: Pairs/small groups.

Different opinions/perspectives: Encourage learners to think about how the opinions and examples of bias come from different perspectives depending on the sources of information used.

Learner response and feedback: Encourage learners to ask each other questions such as:

- Why do you think that's a fact?
- Why do you think that's an opinion?
- Why do think that's an example of bias?

Suggested answers/ideas: Any relevant response depending on the research question learners choose and the information sources they use. Encourage peer feedback to identify what action learners might take to improve their understanding of a fact, opinion and bias, for example, ask you or a peer, or look up definitions and/or examples.

Worked Example for the Main activity

Challenge topic: Digital world or Employment

Suggested research questions:

Digital world

- Is technology creating unemployment?
- Should scientists stop creating robots?
- Does technology bring more advantages than disadvantages to peoples' lives?

Employment

- Is money the main reason people work?
- Is there gender inequality in the workplace?
- Are there more benefits to working than disadvantages?

Independent reflection activity; Self-assessment; Challenge topic review (approx. 15–20 mins)

Good for: Encouraging learners to consider their learning from the lesson, what they think they have done well in terms of working on their own, joining in discussions, asking for help/support, helping their partner, and so on. Encourage learners to reflect on other skills as well as evaluation skills (research, analysis, reflection, communication, collaboration) they have used this lesson, for example, research skills as they searched for information.

Learners also complete the self-assessment to set their own learning targets. Learners think about and shade where they think they are at this time in their learning. 'With help' refers to guidance given (pointing a learner in the right direction, although examples should still come from the learner), for example, from you, other learners, previous work done by the learner in the Learner's Skills Book 7. For the Challenge topic review, learners explore the topic used in this section to develop evaluation skills. These activities can be done in class, at home or in self-study time.

Suggested examples:

3.1 *Evaluate sources, considering the author and purpose, recognising that some sources may be biased.*
For example:

- **Bias** can be seen as favouring a certain side. For example, a waitress in a restaurant thinking the food there is the best in the neighbourhood or someone thinking young people today are disrespectful, unlike when they were younger.
- **A fact** is something that can be proven to be true. For example, from a report or study. Examples: the Earth is round; there are 24 hours in a day.

- **An opinion** is something that can't be proven; it's what someone thinks. For example, red is the best colour; teaching is the best job; Computers are old fashioned.

3.2. *Discuss the effectiveness of a source, making explicit reference to its development of an argument.* An argument is made up of a claim, reasoning and evidence. Being able to identify the elements of an argument: claim (what the author believes), reason(s) (why the author believes this), evidence (how the author knows this).

> Section 4 Reflection

Introduction

The learning objectives and learning goals for reflection skills for Stage 7 focus on the following:

- Personal contribution
- Teamwork
- Personal viewpoints
- Personal learning

However, you might also find opportunities within these lessons to develop some of the other Global Perspectives skills. For example, when considering ways that their personal perspective on an issue may have changed as a result of conducting research or exploring different perspectives, not only will learners be developing reflection skills, they will also be developing their research skills.

The ideas given in this Teacher's Book 7 are suggestions only, and the activities can be used with any of the Global Perspectives topics for Stages 7 to 9, although Worked Examples are provided for some learning activities. It is hoped that the ideas in this Teacher's Book 7 will help you structure your lessons in an active learning way with input from you as the teacher to help guide and support learners to become more reflective learners.

Reflection skills overview

Learning objectives	4.1 Explain personal contribution to teamwork and identify targets for improvement 4.2 Consider the benefits and challenges of teamwork experienced when working together to achieve a shared outcome 4.3 Consider ways that personal perspective on an issue may have changed as a result of conducting research or exploring different perspectives 4.4 Identify skills learned or improved during an activity and relate to personal strengths and areas for improvement
Challenge topic ideas	Human rights; Humans and other species; Tradition, culture and identity; Migration
Key points	• Understanding the difference between the terms 'evaluation' and 'reflection' • Knowing that reflection is about thinking about and considering things deeply • Reflection is a skill that is often used with other skills, such as research (reflecting on what has been found out), evaluation (whether arguments are convincing or courses of action are workable), analysis (proposing courses of action to address an issue, giving reasons for the course(s) of action). Personal perspective needs linking to evidence. Personal opinion is what someone thinks but there is no evidence to support this thinking
Language support	• Pre-teach key vocabulary: reflective learner; praise; criticism; feedback; interrupt; persuade; describe; explain; teamwork; benefits; challenges; contribution; improvement; strengths; limitations.. Also include any topic-specific vocabulary for the Challenge topics – Human rights; Humans and other species; Traditions, culture and identity; migration.

Cross-skills links	1 **Research** 1.2 Identify and begin to reference a range of print and multimedia sources and use them to locate relevant information and answer research questions. 1.3 Select an appropriate method and conduct research to test predictions and begin to answer a research question. 1.4 Select, organise and record relevant information from a range of sources and findings from research, using appropriate methods. 2 **Analysis** 2.1 Identify ideas and evidence from different perspectives within different sources on a given topic. 2.2 Explain how graphical or numerical data supports an argument. 2.3 Explain causes of a local or global issue and the consequences on others. 2.4 Suggest and justify different actions to make a positive difference to a national or global issue. 3 **Evaluation** 3.1 Evaluate sources, considering the author and purpose, recognising that some sources may be biased. 5 **Collaboration** 5.1 The team assign roles and divide tasks fairly, considering the skills of team members and time available, and work together to achieve a shared outcome. 5.2 The team member introduces useful ideas to help achieve a shared outcome and works positively to resolve conflict, solve problems and encourage other team members to participate, when required. 6 **Communication** 6.1 Present information and arguments clearly with some reasoning, referencing sources where appropriate. 6.2 Listen to ideas and information and offer relevant and well-judged contributions that demonstrate understanding of the issue.

Starting with reflection skills: Lesson 1

Lesson 1 focuses on identifying what the term 'reflection' means and identifying personal strengths and areas for development.

CAMBRIDGE STAGE 7 REFLECTION LEARNING OBJECTIVES

4.1 Explain personal contribution to teamwork and identify targets for improvement

4.4 Identify skills learned or improved during an activity and relate to personal strengths and areas for improvement

LEARNING GOALS

To start to:

- understand what the term 'reflection' means
- identify personal strengths
- identify areas for development

How will I know if I reach my goals?

Good for: Learners to give examples of their learning from the lesson. They can complete the table at any point in the lesson, but they might do it at the end.

Resources needed

Learner's Skills Book 7; Challenge topic (e.g. Tradition, culture and identity) and text(s) for the Main activity (see Worked Example for the Main activity); Your own Language Support handout (if appropriate).

Prior learning (approx. 5 mins)

Good for: Building on previous knowledge, learning and understanding. This might be from Primary Global Perspectives, from other subject areas or previous Stage 7 Global Perspectives lessons.

Activity: Define the term 'reflection'. Some might find this a challenge to start with but should be able to gain a better understanding after class discussion. Learners will develop their understanding throughout the section.

Differentiation: Learners work individually, share their ideas in pairs and during class discussion.

Suggested answers: Answers will vary. Reflection is to consider and think deeply about something. This section develops reflection skills about:

- Personal contribution
- Teamwork
- Personal viewpoints
- Personal learning

Not topic specific.

Starter activity (approx. 10 mins)

Good for: Enabling learners to start identifying strengths and weaknesses for learning.

Activity: Learners choose their strengths (they can choose more than one). They should try to explain why they think they have these strengths.

Ways of working: Individual and in pairs feedback.

Suggested answers: Any reasonable and relevant response.

Main activity (approx. 20–25 mins)

Good for: Enabling learners to work together in small groups to share information and develop reflection and communication skills.

Activity: Give each small group a short text. Each member of the group receives the same short text, but the texts for each group are different (see Worked Example). Learners read and discuss their text, making sure that they understand it as they will move groups to tell others about their text.

Differentiation: Group work as support in mixed-ability groups. Choice of text (see Worked Example).

Ways of working: In small groups to start with and then moved into different small groups for sharing.

Different opinions/perspectives: Encourage learners to explore the text(s), noticing the different opinions/viewpoints/perspectives as well as forming their own opinion about what they read.

Learner response and feedback: Encourage learners to focus on the main idea(s) / key points in the text(s). Learners should pay attention to how they are behaving in the groups; refer them back to the Starter activity which asked them to explore their personal strengths. Ask: Are you using these strengths? Could you do more?

Suggested answers/ideas: See Worked Example.

Worked Example for the Main activity

Challenge topic: Tradition, culture and identity

There are four clear paragraphs in the text below. Give each member of the same small group the same paragraph to discuss and note the main idea/key points (10–15 mins). Split the groups so that each new group has someone in it that has discussed each of the four paragraphs. Each member tells the other group members about their paragraph. Learners can make notes in their Learner's Skills Book 7 during or after the discussions.

WHO ARE WE?

1 Mexicans are amongst the happiest people in the world. Our recipe for happiness includes lots of social contact. There's lots of socialising – talking, laughing and joking around. Most families eat together at weekends. My family gatherings include not only mum, dad and us kids, but grandparents, cousins and in-laws as well. We meet at least once a week. Me and my friends go out to eat together, watch sporting activities together and generally enjoy spending time with each other. There is always lots of music and laughter.

2 Being a teenager in China is pretty much like being a teenager anywhere. My alarm clock goes off at 6 a.m. and, before I head out of the door, I have a quick breakfast of bread and milk. By 6.30 a.m. I am on my bike heading off to school, which starts at 7 a.m. and finishes at 5 p.m., which is a long day although I do get to have lunch with grandma in the middle of the day. In the evening, after a family dinner, I have at least an hour of homework to do. If I have some spare time, I love to read. I need to study hard as I want to be a lawyer – a job I think I'll be good at as I love talking!

3 I love living in India. It is a country where people respect the older generation, so much so that extended families living in one house are normal. My grandma has lived with us since I can remember. In India, there is such a mixture of languages, cultures, traditions, cuisines and natural beauty. We all live here together in peace and harmony. I am proud of my heritage. India is the largest democracy in the world. It is more than 5000 years old, and people work hard to make it a better place to live, day by day.

4 America is my home. It's where I'm from. It has soldiers keeping me safe, willing to die to protect me and my family. It has dedicated teachers who love what they do and work hard to help every child succeed. It has doctors and researchers who are doing their best to find cures for diseases. It has millions of hard-working people like my mum who are doing what they need to in order to feed their families and give them a decent standard of living. America is not perfect, but then where is? I don't need it to be perfect because I love it – it's where I belong.

Suggested answers: Each paragraph is about where someone lives and what they think about their homeland. The paragraphs discuss the benefits of living in the country and the culture/traditions of that country.

Independent reflection activity (approx. 5–10 mins)

Good for: Learners to give examples of what personal strengths they used in the lesson and to identify any areas of development. For example, asking questions to clarify thinking a bit more or listening to the ideas of others more before interrupting. Encourage learners to reflect on other skills as well as reflection skills (research, analysis, evaluation, collaboration, communication) they have used this lesson. This activity can be done in class, at home or in self-study time.

Starting with reflection skills: Lesson 2

Lesson 2 focuses on working in a team to achieve a shared outcome and reflecting on the benefits and challenges of teamwork.

CAMBRIDGE STAGE 7 REFLECTION LEARNING OBJECTIVES

4.2 Consider the benefits and challenges of teamwork experienced when working together to achieve a shared outcome

LEARNING GOALS

To start to:

- explain the benefits of teamwork
- work as a team to achieve a shared outcome
- identify the benefits and challenges of teamwork

How will I know if I reach my goals?

Good for: Learners to give examples of their learning from the lesson. They can complete the table at any point in the lesson, but they might do it at the end.

Resources needed

Learner's Skills Book 7; Your own Language Support handout (if appropriate); Challenge topic (e.g. Tradition, culture and identity) and related set of questions for the Main activity (see Worked Example for the Main activity).

Prior learning (approx. 5–10 mins)

Good for: Building on previous knowledge, learning and understanding. This might be from Primary Global Perspectives, from other subject areas, and from their last Global Perspectives lesson.

Activity: Ask learners to consider the qualities/strengths they have identified and which of these are important for teamwork.

Differentiation: Learners can work individually or in pairs.

Suggested answers: Any reasonable and relevant response for reasons why these are all important. Other qualities include: support and respect for each other; taking turns to speak; meeting deadlines; being flexible; knowing who is doing what; keeping each other informed; be a problem-solver; knowing when you are wrong; being willing to take advice and criticism.

Starter activity (approx. 5–10 mins)

Good for: Starting to define what teamwork is and what it is not after discussion about the qualities team members should possess.

Activity: Ask learners to share what they think teamwork is / is not as a class, and then individuals write their own definitions in the Learner's Skills Book 7.

Suggested answers: Any reasonable and relevant response.

Teamwork is when a group of people work together as a whole, towards a shared goal/outcome, with a positive working atmosphere, and supporting each other to combine individual strengths.

Teamwork is not individuals working on their own goal/outcome and then coming together at the end or individuals imposing their own solutions to a team issue, which conflict with the rest of the team's ideas/needs/goals.

Main activity (approx. 20–25 mins)

Good for: Getting teams to work together to discuss an issue/topic to produce an outcome – a diagram of responses to questions.

Activity: Learners discuss and answer the questions as a team. Some questions can be for individuals and some for the whole team, but teams should work together to produce the diagram. The diagram can be a mind map or a spider diagram. (See Worked Example for questions and example diagram.)

Differentiation: List of questions can have some easy questions and some that are more complex. Members of the team support each other.

Ways of working: In teams.

Different opinions/perspectives: Encourage learners to value all the viewpoints/opinions/perspectives explored.

Learner response and feedback: Learners help each other answer questions and decide what information to put in their diagram.

Suggested answers: These will vary according to the topic and questions (see Worked Example).

Worked Example for the Main activity

Challenge topic: Tradition, culture and identity

Questions about identity and community:

1. What nationality are you?
2. What languages do you speak?
3. Where are your parents from?
4. Where are your grandparents from?
5. What is your favourite hobby?
6. What is your favourite food?
7. What is your favourite TV programme?
8. What do you like most about living in your community?
9. What do you like most about being at this school?
10. Do you feel part of the community you live in? Why / Why not?
11. How would you feel if you had to leave your community?
12. How would you feel if you had to leave this school?

Suggested answers: Learners could record their answers to the questions as a mind map. The completed diagram will show who the team is. It's not necessary to record names but just to get an overview of the team's identity. It's important that each diagram captures the main ideas as learners will be using these in Lesson 3 to create a video clip/presentation for others about what it means to be them as a team.

Independent reflection activity (approx. 5–10 mins)

Good for: Encouraging learners to consider the benefits and challenges of working as a team. Ask them to be as honest as they can. Encourage explanation but not all learners will be able to do this. Encourage learners to reflect on other skills as well as reflection skills (research, analysis, evaluation, collaboration, communication) they have used this lesson. This activity can be done in class, at home or in self-study time.

Starting with reflection skills: Lesson 3

Lesson 3 focuses on further understanding of the benefits and challenges of working as a team as teams work towards a shared outcome.

CAMBRIDGE STAGE 7 REFLECTION LEARNING OBJECTIVES

4.1 Explain personal contribution to teamwork and identify targets for improvement

4.2 Consider the benefits and challenges of teamwork experienced when working together to achieve a shared outcome

4.4 Identify skills learned or improved during an activity and relate to personal strengths and areas for improvement

LEARNING GOALS

To start to:

- explain the benefits of teamwork
- explain the challenges of teamwork
- identify contributions to teamwork
- identify areas for improvement in teamwork

How will I know if I reach my goals?

Good for: Learners to give examples of their learning from the lesson. They can complete the table at any point in the lesson, but they might do it at the end.

Resources needed

Learner's Skills Book 7; Challenge topic (e.g. Tradition, culture and identity) and pictures for the Prior learning activity (see Worked Example for the Prior learning activity); notes from the Main activity, Lesson 2 (see Worked Example for the Main activity); Your own Language Support handout (if appropriate).

Prior learning (approx. 5–10 mins)

Good for: Building on previous knowledge, learning and understanding. This might be from Primary Global Perspectives, from other subject areas, or from previous Global Perspectives lessons (particularly Lessons 1 and 2).

Activity: Show all learners two pictures: one of people working together as a team and one of people not working together as a team (see Worked Example for picture ideas). Learners discuss in pairs what each picture shows. Whole-class discussion about the pictures to lead into the Starter activity about the benefits and challenges of teamwork.

Differentiation: Learners work in pairs. Discuss responses in class.

Suggested answers: Any reasonable and relevant response (see Worked Example).

Not topic specific.

Worked Example for the Prior learning activity

Challenge topic: Tradition, culture and identity

Picture suggestions:

Teamwork:

A group of people helping each other climb a mountain:

- https://www.istockphoto.com/gb/photo/group-of-people-on-peak-mountain-climbing-helping-team-work-travel-trekking-success-gm1009803562-272216359

A group of people in a raft working together to help paddle it:

- https://www.istockphoto.com/gb/photo/paddling-a-raft-gm910506822-250747512
- https://www.istockphoto.com/gb/photo/jigsaw-is-a-harmony-among-the-group-will-not-be-impossible-gm1008096704-271942878

Not working as a team: Someone staring at a board of virtual notes in an office on their own.

- https://www.istockphoto.com/gb/photo/woman-sketching-a-business-plan-at-a-creative-office-gm912338074-251168099

Someone working in an office on their own at the computer with all the other computers empty of people.

- https://www.istockphoto.com/gb/photo/these-late-nights-are-killing-me-gm913327640-251414404

Someone working on a computer in an office looking frustrated.

- https://www.istockphoto.com/gb/vector/frustrated-computer-operator-gm505672736-83798669

Suggested answers: Learners discuss what the pictures show (one of people working productively together and another of someone struggling on their own) to initiate discussion about the benefits and challenges of working as a team in the subsequent Starter activity.

Starter activity (approx. 10 mins)

Good for: Exploring and explaining the benefits and challenges of teamwork.

Activity: Learners explain some of the benefits and challenges of working as a team, individually, in pairs and in whole-class discussion.

Differentiation: Some learners will be able to explain three benefits and three challenges, and some will only be able to identify/explain one or two. Pairs can support each other.

Suggested answers: Any reasonable and relevant response.

- **Benefits of teamwork:** more ideas; not struggling alone; mutual support; workload shared equally; can use individual strengths for a collective whole; some tasks can be completed faster, and so on.
- **Challenges of teamwork:** personality clashes; conflict over who does what; not agreeing on ideas; team members absent; team members not as committed to the team as others, and so on.

Not topic specific.

Main activity (approx. 20–25 mins)

Good for: Producing an outcome as a team and reflecting on strengths and areas for improvement.

Activity: Learners plan a team outcome, then write a script with a beginning, middle and end to do with the topic you are studying (information gained from answering the questions in the Main activity, Lesson 2). See Worked Example. Once learners have the script, they can create an outcome, i.e. record it as a video clip, audio with posters or presentation.

Differentiation: Learners work as a team, with team roles and responsibilities according to their strengths. Discuss the various roles and responsibilities. (See Worked Example.)

Ways of working: Whole-class explanation of task. In teams (teacher choice or friendship groups). Teams should be the same as for the Main activity, Lesson 2.

Different opinions/perspectives: Stress that the information presented should explore the views/opinions/perspectives of the whole team.

Learner response and feedback: Learners ask each other questions as they are working as a team:

- Do we know what the purpose of the ... is?
- Is the purpose of the ... clear?
- Which information should we use and why?
- Which information should we discard and why?
- Is the ... suitable for the identified audience (e.g. our peers; younger learners)?
- What's good about the ... (strengths)?
- What's not so good about the ... (limitations)?

They also evaluate another team's script in terms of its strengths and areas for improvement.

Suggested answers: Answers will vary according to the topic chosen. Teams might also produce different outcomes, and each team will have gathered different information according to the questions given and answered in the Main activity, Lesson 2 (see Worked Example).

Worked Example for the Main activity

Challenge topic: Tradition, culture and identity

Learners create an outcome (e.g. video clip) to show others who their team is and give some information about the team. Learners write the script as a team and then shoot the video clip as a team if possible. If not, they can create a presentation or posters. To start with, they might introduce themselves (name, age, school they go to) before they focus on where each member comes from, the interests of each member of team, their culture, language and some traditions linked to this, and so on. To end, they might say why they work together well as a team or what they might need to improve upon.

Purpose: To show others who the team is, where each member comes from and what's important to them (see questions from Lesson 2).

Audience: Peers in the same class.

Outcome: Video clip / audio recording with posters, presentation.

My role: For example: script writer, editor, camera operator, cue card holder, credits, reporter, props/equipment organiser (learners may all contribute to the script and then have another role once it comes to filming).

Independent reflection activity Self-assessment; Challenge topic review (approx. 15–20 mins)

Good for: Encouraging learners to consider their learning in lessons and answers go towards achieving the learning objectives for reflection skills.

Learners also complete the self-assessment to set their own learning targets before they move on. Learners think about and shade where they think they are at this time in their learning. 'With help' refers to guidance given (pointing a learner in the right direction, although examples should still come from learners), for example, from you, other learners, previous work done by the learner in the Learner's Skills Book 7. For the Challenge topic review, learners explore the topic used in this section to develop reflection skills. These activities can be done in class, at home or in self-study time.

Suggested examples:

4.1 *Explain personal contribution to teamwork and identify targets for improvement.* Example: 'My personal contribution was helping with the script as I'm good at writing in English. I was also the editor because of my ability in spelling. I need to listen to what others say more so that it helps my own understanding. I also need to ask more questions if I don't understand something.'

4.2 *Consider the benefits and challenges of teamwork experienced when working together to achieve a shared outcome.* For example:

- **Benefits of teamwork:** more ideas; not struggling alone; mutual support; workload shared equally; can use individual strengths for a collective whole; some tasks can be completed faster, and so on.
- **Challenges of teamwork**: personality clashes; conflict over who does what; not agreeing on ideas; team members absent; team members not as committed to the team as others, and so on.

4.4 *Identify skills learned or improved during an activity and relate to personal strengths and areas for improvement.* For example: 'Writing, listening, reflecting, evaluating as I could see a strength and a limitation of the video clip. A strength was that it was clear from the video how much we had in common. A limitation was that we didn't really talk about how we would feel if we didn't belong to our community.'

Developing reflection skills: Lesson 4

Lesson 4 focuses on working as a team to gain information by planning and conducting research.

CAMBRIDGE STAGE 7 REFLECTION LEARNING OBJECTIVES

4.1 Explain personal contribution to teamwork and identify targets for improvement

LEARNING GOALS

To develop knowledge and understanding about:

- what I contribute to teamwork
- how to improve my contribution to teamwork

How will I know if I reach my goals?

Good for: Learners to give examples of their learning from the lesson. They can complete the table at any point in the lesson, but they might do it at the end.

Resources needed

Learner's Skills Book 7; Your own Language Support handout (if appropriate); Challenge topic for the starter and main activities (e.g. Tradition, culture and identity); internet access; website addresses for the Main activity (see Worked Example for the Main activity).

Prior learning (approx. 5–10 mins)

Good for: Building on previous knowledge, learning and understanding. This might be from Primary Global Perspectives, from other subject areas, or from previous Stage 7 Global Perspectives lessons (particularly Lessons 1–3).

Activity: Review the challenges and benefits of teamwork. You can write these down and discuss them. Try to elicit suggestions for how to overcome the challenges and end discussion on the benefits as learners will continue to work in teams in subsequent lessons.

Differentiation: Allow learners to look back in their Learner's Skills Book 7. Some will not need to. Learners can work in pairs for support. Target learners for responses in class discussion.

Suggested answers: Any reasonable and relevant response.

- **Challenges of teamwork:** Personality clashes; conflict over who does what; not agreeing on ideas; team members absent; team members not as committed to the team as others, and so on.
- **Benefits of teamwork:** More ideas; not struggling alone; mutual support; workload shared equally; can use individual strengths for a collective whole; some tasks can be completed faster, and so on.

Not topic specific.

Starter activity (approx. 10 mins)

Good for: Reviewing topic-specific vocabulary.

Activity: Learners brainstorm as many words and phrases as they can to do with the topic.

Ways of working: Individually, in pairs and small-group discussion.

Suggested answers: Depends on the topic.

Not topic specific, but words/phrases will be useful for the Main activity.

Main activity (approx. 20–25 mins)

Good for: Planning to do and conducting research as part of a team.

Activity:

1 Learners decide who is researching what and which website addresses they are going to use. These can be given to learners by the teacher (see Worked Example for suggestions). They complete the table. There is space for five learners per team but an optimum number is four in a team.

2 Once they have decided who is researching what, each learner makes notes about what they want to find out (see Worked Example for suggestions). Next to the notes, they ask a question and then have space to record an answer. .

Differentiation: Learners can work in pairs for support. They could use a graphic organiser to organise thoughts (see Worked Example).

Ways of working: Individually or in pairs to share ideas and clarify own thinking. Individual/pair research as part of a whole team project.

Different opinions/perspectives: Learners will be finding ideas/information from different opinions/perspectives.

Learner response and feedback: Encourage learners to help and support each other in teams. They can ask questions such as:

- What are you trying to find out?
- Are you looking in the right place?
- Have you tried the suggested website(s)?
- Have you tried to use just one or two websites rather than lots?
- Have you noted the website address?
- Do you have a question you want an answer to?

Suggested answers: Depends on the topic chosen (see Worked Example).

Worked Example for the Main activity

Challenge topic: Tradition, culture and identity

Learners can research different communities and/or different groups of people. For example, the Gond tribe in India: https://www.everyculture.com/wc/Germany-to-Jamaica/Gonds.html

	Notes (What I want to find out about?)	Question	Answer
1	Language	What language do they speak?	Gondi (Also: Hindi, Marathi or Telegu)
2	Food	Do they eat the same kinds of food as me?	Two types of grain called kodo and kutki, vegetables and honey
3	Traditions	What different traditions are there?	Arts such as pottery and basket making; celebrate festive occasions (worshipping Gods) with song and dance
4	Identity	Which cultural group do they belong to?	Tribal, the largest in India, Hindus
5	Work	What jobs do they do?	Farmers; some landowners

Other groups:

- Syrian refugees in Britain (https://fullfact.org/immigration/syrian-refugees-uk)
- Australian aboriginal tribe Anangu Pitjantjatjara (https://www.naturalresources.sa.gov.au/alinytjara-wilurara/visiting/landscapes/southern-apy)
- Māori people in New Zealand (https://www.newzealand.com/us/maori-culture)
- New Orleaners in America (https://www.neworleans.com/things-to-do/history/people-and-culture-of-new-orleans)

Each member of the team should research a different community so that they can share what they have learned in subsequent lessons.

Independent reflection activity (approx. 5–10 mins)

Good for: Encouraging learners to consider their learning from the lesson. Encourage learners to reflect on other skills (research, analysis, evaluation, collaboration, communication) they have used this lesson, as well as reflection skills. This activity can be done in class, at home or in self-study time.

Developing reflection skills: Lesson 5

Lesson 5 focuses on learners working in teams to create questionnaires for others to find out information to inform their own perspective.

CAMBRIDGE STAGE 7 REFLECTION LEARNING OBJECTIVES

4.3 Consider ways that personal perspective on an issue may have changed as a result of conducting research or exploring different perspectives

4.4 Identify skills learned or improved during an activity and relate to personal strengths and areas for improvement

LEARNING GOALS

To develop knowledge and understanding about:

- what a personal perspective is
- skills learned or improved

How will I know if I reach my goals?

Good for: Learners to give examples of their learning from the lesson. They can complete the table at any point in the lesson, but they might do it at the end.

Resources needed

Learner's Skills Book 7; Your own Language Support handout (if appropriate); internet access; Challenge topic for the starter and main activities (e.g. Tradition, culture and identity); topic pictures for the Starter activity (see Worked Example for the Starter activity)

Prior learning (approx. 5–10 mins)

Good for: Building on previous knowledge, learning and understanding. This might be from Primary Global Perspectives, from other subject areas, or from previous Stage 7 Global Perspectives lessons (particularly Lesson 4).

Activity: Review learning about the difference between a local perspective and a personal perspective.

Differentiation: Allow learners to look back in their Learner's Skills Book 7. Some will not need to. Learners can discuss or work individually and then share ideas with a partner/whole class.

Suggested answers: Any reasonable and relevant response.

- **A local perspective:** Relates to a specific community/locality/school, is evident by what people think/believe about something (possibly due to culture and traditions) and is based on the needs and issues of the whole community.
- **A personal perspective:** What an individual thinks about something depending on their upbringing/education, and what they have learned from various sources throughout their life to form their perspective.

Starter activity (approx. 10 mins)

Good for: Generating questions using the question stem words.

Activity: Learners create questions relevant to the topic/picture the teacher shows them (see Worked Example).

Ways of working: Individually, in pairs and whole-class discussion.

Suggested answers: Depends on topic/picture (see Worked Example).

Worked Example for the Starter activity

Challenge topic: Tradition, culture and identity

Picture suggestions:

- Women carrying food: https://www.istockphoto.com/gb/photo/indian-women-carrying-food-gm183406824-15606219
- Tribe: https://www.istockphoto.com/gb/photo/tribes-of-odisha-gm1016628782-273485075
- Refugee children in a crowded refugee camp: https://www.istockphoto.com/gb/photo/syrian-children-in-crowded-refugee-camp-gm458886393-23281686

Suggested questions:

Will depend on the photo used.

- What's happening?
- When do you think the photo was taken?
- Where do you think this is?
- Who do you think these people are?
- How do you think this situation happened?
- Why do you think they are doing this?

Main activity (approx. 20–25 mins)

Good for: Generating questions and answers about a topic/issue.

Activity: In Lesson 5, each team will discuss their research and write ten questions for another team to find the answers to. In Lesson 6, teams will answer each others' questions. Learners continue to work individually to generate their own questions. They might need to do some further research to find the answers to these questions. They then join their team mates and choose the best ten questions (encourage a variety of stem questions such as 'why' and 'how', and not just 'what' questions). They will be sharing these questions with another team in Lesson 6.

Differentiation: Learners work in teams to write suitable questions. They will also need to know the answers to give feedback to another team in Lesson 6.

Ways of working: Individually and then in teams to choose and write questions (encourage teamwork by reviewing the benefits of working as a team and some of the rules: taking turns, listening to each other, etc.)

Different opinions/perspectives: Learners are exploring ideas from different perspectives to write and answer the questions.

Learner response and feedback: Encourage learners to discuss in teams the quality of the questions and whether they can be answered.

Suggested answers: Learners are developing their ability to ask and answer questions and to form a personal perspective as they discuss which questions to use from each member of the team. Answers depend on the questions and research resources used.

Independent reflection activity (approx. 5–10 mins)

Good for: Encouraging learners to reflect on their own learning from the lesson and the skills they have learned or improved in the lesson. This activity can be done in class, at home or in self-study time.

Developing reflection skills: Lesson 6

Lesson 6 follows on from lesson 5. Learners focus on answering questions about a topic/ issue and identifying how a personal perspective can change or develop after research.

CAMBRIDGE STAGE 7 REFLECTION LEARNING OBJECTIVES

4.3 Consider ways that personal perspective on an issue may have changed as a result of conducting research or exploring different perspectives

LEARNING GOALS

To develop knowledge and understanding about:

- what a personal perspective is
- how to explain my personal perspective

How will I know if I reach my goals?

Good for: Learners to give examples of their learning from the lesson. They can complete the table at any point in the lesson, but they might do it at the end.

Resources needed

Learner's Skills Book 7; Your own Language Support handout (if appropriate); internet access; Challenge topic for the starter and main activities (e.g. Tradition, culture and identity, but any topic suitable); listening text (video clip, podcast) for the Starter activity (see Worked Example for the Starter activity).

Prior learning (approx. 5–10 mins)

Good for: Building on previous knowledge, learning and understanding. This might be from Primary Global Perspectives, from other subject areas, or from previous Stage 7 Global Perspectives lessons.

Activity: Review learning about question words and why asking a variety of questions when doing research is important.

Differentiation: Learners can work in pairs for support and share ideas with another pair.

Suggested answers: Any reasonable and relevant response. Different types of question gain different answers. Some enable short, specific, more fact-based answers (what, when, where, who) and some require answers that need thinking about (why, how) and are likely to produce more analysis, giving more detail and ideas from different perspectives.

Starter activity (approx. 5–10 mins)

Good for: Exploring what a personal perspective is and how it might change/develop according to experiences and what the individual finds important.

Activity: Play a clip for the learners to listen to. Decide which perspective the ideas in the clip come from. The clip should present ideas from a personal perspective. Any clip can be used (see Worked Example for ideas).

Ways of working: Individual, in pairs and whole-class discussion.

Suggested answers: Depends on the clip watched/listened to (see Worked Example).

Worked Example for the Starter activity

Challenge topic: Tradition, culture and identity

1 Vlog about someone's experiences at Konark festival, India:

https://www.youtube.com/watch?v=hY0yLOP5S9o

Questions to ask:

- Which perspective are the ideas in this clip from: global, national/local or personal? *Personal*
- What does the author find important? *Food, activities on and in the water, Konark temple are all mentioned and shown in the clip.*

2 Video clip about someone's trip to India (first 5 mins):

https://www.youtube.com/watch?v=5pkc7wxCR2A

Questions to ask:

- Which perspective are the ideas in this clip from: global, national/local or personal? *Personal*
- What is the personal perspective of the author? *That India is crazy and colourful; it's a noisy, overwhelming place; the food is amazing*
- What evidence is provided for this perspective? *Photos of main bazaar road; rickshaw journey/ traffic jam; spice market; street food.*

3 Video clip about first impressions of China:

https://www.youtube.com/watch?v=kVGFMqHrfSY (from about 3 mins onwards)

Questions to ask:

- Which perspective are the ideas in this clip from: global, national/local or personal? *Personal*
- What is/are the personal perspective(s) of the author? *It's expensive; people are genuine; different ways of thinking/cultural differences*
- What evidence is provided for this/these perspective (s)? *Own experiences of being in China, arriving in China and living in China.*

Main activity (approx. 20–25 mins)

Good for: Finding out information about a topic/issue by answering questions.

Activity: Teams answer the questions created by another team in Lesson 5. Encourage members of teams to work together. Each team member can take two or three questions and focus on researching the answers to these. They then come together as a team to discuss all the answers and what they have found out.

Differentiation: Learners can work in pairs for support to answer their allotted questions.

Ways of working: Individually or in pairs as support, and as a team so that all members of the team know the answers to all the questions.

Different opinions/perspectives: The activity focuses on answering questions and it's likely that learners will come across ideas from different perspectives within different information sources.

Learner response and feedback: Learners encourage each other by asking questions: Which question are you answering? How are you getting on? Is there something you're struggling with? How can I help?

Suggested answers: Answers will vary according to the questions.

Independent reflection activity; Self-assessment; Challenge topic review (approx. 15–20 mins)

Good for: Encouraging learners to reflect on their understanding of 'personal perspective' and to give an example from the Challenge topic.

Learners also complete the self-assessment to set their own learning targets before they move on. Learners think about and shade where they think they are at this time in their learning. 'With help' refers to guidance given (pointing a learner in the right direction, although examples should still come from learners), for example, from you, other learners, previous work done by the learner in the Learner's Skills Book 7. For the Challenge topic review, learners explore the topic used in this section to develop reflection skills. These activities can be done in class, at home or in self-study time.

Suggested examples:

4.1 *Explain personal contribution to teamwork and identify targets for improvement.* Example: 'My personal contribution was creating some questions for others to find the answers to. I also needed to know the answers, so I had to do some research too. I needed to take more of a leadership role when deciding which questions to use for our team.'

4.2 *Consider the benefits and challenges of teamwork experienced when working together to achieve a shared outcome.* For example:

- **Benefits of teamwork:** more ideas; not struggling alone; mutual support; workload shared equally; can use individual strengths for a collective whole; some tasks can be completed faster, and so on.
- **Challenges of teamwork**: personality clashes; conflict over who does what; not agreeing on ideas; team members absent; team members not as committed to the team as others, and so on.

4.3 *Consider ways that personal perspective on an issue may have changed as a result of conducting research or exploring different perspectives.* A personal perspective is what you think about a topic/issue as a result of your experiences and what you learn from others and from research. Your personal perspective can change or develop as you become more informed about a topic or issue. Example: 'I used to think that it would be great to be part of a tribe that didn't have to go to school or work. Now, I think that the way of life is difficult as it's hard work farming the land for food to survive.'

4.4 *Identify skills learned or improved during an activity and relate to personal strengths and areas for improvement.* Example: 'I am getting better at analysis as I could write a question and answer about why Syrian refugees had to leave their homes. I need to improve my ability to work on my own more as I rely on my partner for support a lot in class, even though I can work confidently on my own at home.'

Getting better at reflection skills: Lesson 7

Lesson 7 focuses on working as a team to discuss and plan a course of action to address an issue.

CAMBRIDGE STAGE 7 REFLECTION LEARNING OBJECTIVES

4.1 Explain personal contribution to teamwork and identify targets for improvement

4.2 Consider the benefits and challenges of teamwork experienced when working together to achieve a shared outcome

4.4 Identify skills learned or improved during an activity and relate to personal strengths and areas for improvement

LEARNING GOALS

To get better at:

- knowing that my personal strengths can benefit teamwork
- working with others towards a shared outcome
- identifying skills learned/improved

How will I know if I reach my goals?

Good for: Learners to give examples of their learning from the lesson. They can complete the table at any point in the lesson, but they might do it at the end.

Resources needed

Learner's Skills Book 7; Your own Language Support handout (if appropriate); internet access; Challenge topic (e.g. Human rights) and picture related to a topic issue for the Starter activity (see Worked Example for the Starter activity); Worked Example from Section 2 'Analysis', Lesson 4 for scaffolding/modelling; Challenge topic for the Main activity (e.g. Migration).

Prior learning (approx. 5–10 mins)

Good for: Building on previous knowledge, learning and understanding. This might be from Primary Global Perspectives, from other subject areas, or from previous Stage 7 Global Perspectives lessons.

Activity: Review own personal strengths.

Differentiation: Allow thinking time. Learners can choose more than one option but advise them that they will need to give an example for each one chosen. Learners add other strengths after class discussion.

Suggested answers: Any reasonable and relevant examples.

Own ideas: Good at listening; planning; leading; working on my own; working in a team; helping others; asking 'why' questions. Can also be examples from outside the classroom.

Not topic specific.

Starter activity (approx. 10 mins)

Good for: Reviewing issues and what to consider when looking at courses of action to help resolve issues.

Activity: Show picture(s) related to an issue. Elicit the issue(s) from learners and what they know about it. Discuss steps to find a course of action to help resolve the issue. Either elicit from learners without help or give them the steps to consider their importance. You can also refer them to the tips. Whole-class discussion to clarify thinking and gain new learning.

Suggested ideas: See Worked Example.

Not topic specific.

Worked Example for the Starter activity

Challenge topic: Human rights

Picture ideas for issues to propose courses of action for:

- Children looking lost/not at school: https://www.istockphoto.com/gb/photo/children-pose-on-the-sunny-village-market-gm532279184-94198999
- Children in a crowded classroom: https://www.thenewhumanitarian.org/photo/200802228/children-crowded-class-moto-primary-school-molo-town-rift-valley-province-kenya
- Syrian refugee children who should be in school: https://ourworld.unu.edu/en/education-in-emergencies-will-syrian-refugee-children-become-a-lost-generation

Steps to developing a course of action:

- Identify the issue. (What is the issue? It is important that learners understand that it is something that has a course of action to help resolve it.)
- Explain the issue. (For whom is it an issue? Why is it an issue?)
- Search for and organise information. (What information do I need? Where do I get this information? Primary and/or secondary research sources?)
- Check the resources needed. (Is my course of action realistic? What do I need to implement it?)
- Check whether the course of action is SMART – Specific, Measurable, Achievable, Realistic and Time-bound
- Form a plan. (Who does what and when?)
- Evaluate the course of action. (Does my course of action help resolve the issue?).

Main activity (approx. 20–25 mins)

Good for: Working in teams to discuss and plan a course of action to address an issue.

Activity: Complete the table as a team for the issue given (see Worked Example) and decide on the best course of action ready for Lesson 8.

Differentiation: Review the Worked Example from Section 2 'Analysis', Lesson 4 with the whole class. Elicit understanding about how to generate courses of action for issues. Learners work in mixed-ability teams.

Ways of working: Whole class for modelling and then in teams.

Different opinions/perspectives: Encourage learners to consider the issue from different perspectives to arrive at a suitable course of action.

Learner response and feedback: Encourage learners to ask each other questions such as:

- Is this course of action specific/related to the issue?
- Is this course of action measurable? How can we tell if it works?
- Is this course of action achievable? Are we going to be able to do it?
- Is this course of action realistic (given our situation, the resources we have, etc.)?
- Is this course of action achievable in the time we have?

Suggested answers/ideas: See Worked Example.

Worked Example for the Main activity

Challenge topic: Migration

Example Issue: What can we do to help refugees settle into our school?

Possible course of action 1: Have lessons in their language.

- **Reasons for/against:** Difficult to do; need to involve the whole school; would need to be taken out of classes as other students don't speak that language.
- **Other:** Who to involve? How time consuming? How to get resources translated? What about other students? Who teaches them?

Possible course of action 2: Produce an audio recording with some key phrases translated into the language.

- **Reasons for/against:** Easy to do; can involve students; reach a wide audience – students and parents.
- **Other:** Who to involve? Who does what? What phrases to use? Resources needed?

Possible course of action 3: Produce a leaflet/brochure with key information about the school; a map of where the main areas in the school are; lessons/ subjects and a brief overview for the term/year; timings (start and end of day and breaks); holiday dates; canteen arrangement and food choices; timetable; after school activities; who to contact for different reasons and contact details, and so on.

- **Reasons for/against:** Easy to do; can be done individually or in teams; in class.

- **Other:** Who to involve – need permissions (class teacher and Head Teacher), decide on who does what, resources needed, time frame.

Independent reflection activity (approx. 5–10 mins)

Good for: Encouraging learners to consider their learning from the lesson, specifically a skill they have improved. This might be communicating – joining in discussions, reflection and evaluation – thinking about the strengths and limitations of possible courses of action, and so on. Encourage learners to reflect on other skills (research, analysis, evaluation, collaboration, communication) they have used this lesson, as well as reflection skills. This activity can be done in class, at home or in self-study time.

Getting better at reflection skills: Lesson 8

Lesson 8 continues the sequence from Lesson 7 and focuses on working in teams to plan and produce a team outcome after deciding on a course of action to help resolve an issue.

CAMBRIDGE STAGE 7 REFLECTION LEARNING OBJECTIVES

4.1 Explain personal contribution to teamwork and identify targets for improvement

4.4 Identify skills learned or improved during an activity and relate to personal strengths and areas for improvement

LEARNING GOALS

To get better at:

- explaining what my contribution to teamwork is
- identifying what I have learned/improved
- identifying areas for further development

How will I know if I reach my goals?

Good for: Learners to give examples of their learning from the lesson. They can complete the table at any point in the lesson, but they might do it at the end.

Resources needed

Learner's Skills Book 7; Your own Language Support handout (if appropriate); internet access; Challenge topic for the Main activity (e.g. Migration/Human rights); scaffolding plan (see Worked Example for the Main activity); Resources to create team outcome (paper/pens).

Prior learning (approx. 5 mins)

Good for: Building on previous knowledge, learning and understanding. This might be from Primary Global Perspectives, from other subject areas, or from previous Stage 7 Global Perspectives lessons (especially Lesson 7).

Activity: Review learning about courses of action from Lesson 7 and what needs considering when proposing a course of action.

Differentiation: Learners work in teams.

Suggested answers/ideas: A course of action is a plan or method for achieving a specific aim or goal and might involve producing an outcome like a video or a presentation. A course of action might also be an event like a cake sale to raise money for a particular cause. Learners need to consider:

- Is this course of action specific/explicitly related to the issue?
- Is this course of action measurable? How can we tell if it works?
- Is this course of action achievable? Are we going to be able to do it?
- Is this course of action realistic (sensible given our situation and the resources we have, etc.)?
- Is this course of action achievable in the time we have?

Not topic specific.

Starter activity (approx. 10 mins)

Good for: Reviewing suggestions for courses of action from Lesson 7.

Activity: Learners discuss and answer the questions about the course of action they decided on in Lesson 7. They should answer yes/no and then give an explanation. They should come up with a team outcome for this course of action – for example, a video clip or podcast with a series of pictures. They should check their idea for their team outcome with you.

Suggested answers:

a Is it specific to the issue? Yes, as it focuses on helping to ...

b Is it measurable? Yes, as we can ask for feedback from ... to see if it helped ...

c Is it achievable? Yes, we can do it in class and after school if necessary.

d Is it realistic? Yes, as we have all the resources.

e Can you do it in the time allowed? Yes, we have the rest of this lesson, the next lesson and some home study time when we can meet.

Main activity (approx. 20–25 mins)

Good for: Planning and designing a team outcome in teams.

Activity: Learners plan to complete their team outcome and start to complete it. Discuss who does what and when. See Worked Example for a completed plan.

Once they have their plan, learners can complete their team outcome. They can use some of this lesson and some of Lesson 9 to complete it. Encourage learners to make amendments according to areas for improvement suggested in the peer feedback.

Differentiation: Learners work in teams. Encourage teams to allocate tasks according to personal strengths.

Ways of working: In teams/small groups.

Different opinions/perspectives: Encourage learners to consider the audience for their team outcome as they plan and complete it.

Learner response and feedback: Encourage learners to give feedback to each other as they are completing their team outcome. Some questions to ask:

- Is that part clear?
- Do we need to add ... ?
- Do you think there's too much/too little information about ... ?
- Would it be better to put ... ?
- Is it suitable for ... ?

Learners can also give peer feedback on each other's plans as they are completed as well as feedback on the final team outcome.

Suggested answers: See Worked Example for planning to complete a leaflet to help settle refugees into school. Learners can pass their outcome to another team for peer feedback; answering the questions in the Learner's Skills Book 7.

Worked Example for the Main activity

Challenge topic: Migration/Human rights

Issue	How can we help refugees settle better into our school community?			
Course of action	To produce something that has the key information about our school in it for newcomers to the school to find their way around more easily.			
Team outcome	Leaflet with key information for newcomers to school.			
Team members	Hans, Joe, Mayte, Kelly			
Start date	**Completion date**	**Task (What?) Action (How?)**	**Person responsible**	**Resources needed**
21/03	28/03	T: Timetable, holiday dates & lessons A: Ask Assistant Principal	Hans & Joe	Pen & notepad
21/03	28/03	T: Key phrases A: Ask neighbours for translation	Joe & Kelly	Phone to record phrases, pen & notepad
21/03	28/03	T: Food in canteen A: Interview dinner staff	Mayte & Kelly	Pen & notepad
21/03	28/03	T: After school activities A: Ask sports, art and music staff	Hans & Mayte	Pen & notepad
28/03	04/03	T: Create leaflet from research A: On computer	All – as per research done Kelly – intro to leaflet (purpose) and key phrases Joe – timetable, holiday dates and lessons Hans – after school activities Mayte – food choices/canteen	Computer, paper, printer

Independent reflection activity (approx. 5–10 mins)

Good for: Encouraging learners to consider their learning from the lesson, their individual contribution to the teamwork, what they learned and what they needed help with. This activity can be done in class, at home or in self-study time.

Getting better at reflection skills: Lesson 9

Lesson 9 follows on from Lesson 8. Learners complete their team outcome and reflect on the benefits and challenges of teamwork and their personal perspective.

CAMBRIDGE STAGE 7 REFLECTION LEARNING OBJECTIVES

4.2 Consider the benefits and challenges of teamwork experienced when working together to achieve a shared outcome

4.3 Consider ways that personal perspective on an issue may have changed as a result of conducting research or exploring different perspectives

LEARNING GOALS

To get better at:

- describing some of the benefits of teamwork
- describing some of the challenges of teamwork
- explaining how my personal perspective has changed/developed

How will I know if I reach my goals?

Good for: Learners to give examples of their learning from the lesson. They can complete the table at any point in the lesson, but they might do it at the end.

Resources needed

Learner's Skills Book 7; Your own Language Support handout (if appropriate); completed plan from Lesson 8; computers; resources to complete team outcome.

Prior learning (approx. 5 mins)

Good for: Building on previous knowledge, learning and understanding. This might be from Primary Global Perspectives, from other subject areas, or from previous Stage 7 Global Perspectives lessons (particularly Lesson 8).

Activity: Discuss the challenges of teamwork. Take this opportunity to suggest ways of addressing these challenges. Ask for learners' input.

Differentiation: Learners work in teams for this activity.

Suggested answers:

2 Listen to each other; take turns; meet deadlines; divide up the tasks further; support and help each other; ask questions; be more organised; have a leader; respect the team; state ideas clearly; compromise; ask your teacher, and so on.

Not topic specific.

Starter activity (approx. 10 mins)

Good for: Reviewing peer feedback about the team outcome.

Activity: Teams work together to review their team outcome after peer feedback. They identify changes they need to make for the team outcome to be more effective.

Suggested answers: Specific to the topic for Lessons 7–9.

Main activity (approx. 20–25 mins)

Good for: Evaluating a team outcome.

Activity: Learners work in teams. They finish their team outcome taking account of any changes identified as a result of peer feedback. They can use the checklist to evaluate their team outcome and once completed, can ask another team to evaluate their team outcome.

Differentiation: Learners work in teams.

Ways of working: Small groups to develop teamworking skills.

Different opinions/perspectives: Encourage learners to evaluate their team outcome from the perspective of their target audience for their team outcome.

Learner response and feedback: Encourage learners to give feedback to each other using the questions from the checklist and in 'Tips'.

Suggested ideas: See Worked Example.

Worked Example for the Main activity

Challenge topic: Migration/Human rights

Evaluating a team outcome

1. Advise looking back to see if the team outcome addresses/answers the question.
2. Learners explain how it can help to resolve the issue, for example, by making refugee students feel more integrated/part of the community.
3. Judge how much work is needed to finish the team outcome and decide whether to finish it or not depending on answers to the first two questions.
4. Learners make a judgement based on answers to questions 1–3.
5. Learners decide the longevity of their team outcome, for example, the details of the timetable and lessons might need changing. A decision needs to be taken as to when to update it and who does what to update it.

Learners might come up with other questions to evaluate their team outcome, for example, Is the content clear? Is it suitable for the age and experience of the audience? Is it helpful (ask the audience)?

Independent reflection activity; Self-assessment; Challenge topic review (approx. 15–20 mins)

Good for: Encouraging learners to consider their thoughts about what reflection is and how these might have changed whilst completing this section, giving reasons for this change.

Learners also complete the self-assessment to set their own learning targets. Learners think about and shade where they think they are at this time in their learning. 'With help' refers to guidance given (pointing a learner in the right direction, although examples should still come from learners), for example, from you, other learners, previous work done by the learner in the Learner's Skills Book 7. For the Challenge topic review, learners explore the topic used in this section to develop reflection skills. These activities can be done in class, at home or in self-study time.

Suggested examples:

4.1 *Explain personal contribution to teamwork and identify targets for improvement.* Example: 'My personal contribution was asking the dinner staff about the food they serve in the canteen and whether there would be a chance to serve at least one Middle-Eastern dish per day to make the refugees feel more at home. I also created the page that listed the foods served in the canteen. I needed to ask for more guidance at the start as to what I was supposed to be doing as I was a little unclear.'

4.2 *Consider the benefits and challenges of teamwork experienced when working together to achieve a shared outcome.* For example:

- **Benefits of teamwork:** more ideas; not struggling alone; mutual support; workload shared equally; can use individual strengths for a collective whole; some tasks can be completed faster, and so on.
- **Challenges of teamwork**: personality clashes; conflict over who does what; not agreeing on ideas; team members absent; team members not as committed to the team as others, and so on.
- **Ways of working more effectively**: listen to each other; take turns; meet deadlines; divide up the tasks further; support and help each other; ask questions; be more organised; have a leader; respect the team; state ideas clearly; compromise; ask the teacher.

4.3 *Consider ways that personal perspective on an issue may have changed as a result of conducting research or exploring different perspectives.* A personal perspective is what you think about a topic/issue as a result of your experiences and what you learn from others and from research. Your personal perspective can change or develop as you become more informed about a topic or issue. Example: 'I used to think that teenagers in Syria ate different things to me, but I now think that teenagers around the world eat similar things. This is because of the research I have done about Syrian refugees and from talking to the Syrian refugees in school who say they love hamburgers.'

4.4 *Identify skills learned or improved during an activity and relate to personal strengths and areas for improvement.* Example: 'I am getting better at evaluating as I could see what needed changing in our team outcome and why we needed to change it. I must get better at communicating my thoughts though and tell others so that we can have a better team outcome that addresses the issue more.'

Section 5 Collaboration

Introduction

The learning objectives and learning goals for collaboration skills for Stage 7 focus on:

- Cooperation and interdependence
- Engaging in teamwork

However, you might also find opportunities within these lessons to develop some of the other Global Perspectives skills. For example, when completing teamwork, not only will learners be developing collaboration skills, it is likely that they will also be developing their reflection skills.

The ideas given in this Teacher's Book 7 are suggestions only, and the activities can be used with any of the Global Perspectives topics for Stages 7 to 9, although Worked Examples are provided for some learning activities. It is hoped that the ideas in this Teacher's Book 7 will help you structure your lessons in an active learning way with input from you as the teacher to help guide and support learners to become more collaborative learners.

Collaboration skills overview

Learning objectives	5.1 The team assign roles and divide tasks fairly, considering the skills of team members and time available, and work together to achieve a shared outcome 5.2 The team member introduces useful ideas to help achieve a shared outcome and works positively to resolve conflict, solve problems and encourage other team members to participate, when required
Challenge topic ideas	Water, food and agriculture; Trade and aid; Language and communication
Key points	• Understanding the terms 'fact', 'opinion', 'prediction' and 'bias' • Realising that collaboration is about working together as a team towards a shared outcome, and not simply sitting in a team and working independently • Understanding that individual strengths lead to effective teamwork • Knowing that effective teamwork relies on the participation and contributions of the whole team • Understanding that conflict in teams is normal and knowing some strategies to avoid/resolve conflict for effective teamwork • Appreciating the importance of feedback to develop learning and skills
Language support	• Pre-teach key vocabulary: collaboration; fact; opinion; prediction; bias; relevant; compromise; shared outcome; argument; presentation; perspective; relevant; supported; structure; conflict; resolve; valid; combined; critical; feedback; highlights; areas for improvement.. Also include any topic-specific vocabulary for the Challenge topics – Water, food and agriculture; Trade and aid; Language and communication.

<table>
<tr><td rowspan="1">Cross-skills links</td><td>
1 Research
1.1 Construct relevant research questions.
1.2 Identify and begin to reference a range of print and multimedia sources and use them to locate relevant information and answer research questions.
1.3 Select an appropriate method and conduct research to test predictions and begin to answer a research question.
1.4 Select, organise and record relevant information from a range of sources and findings from research, using appropriate methods.
2 Analysis
2.1 Identify ideas and evidence from different perspectives within different sources on a given topic.
2.2 Explain how graphical or numerical data supports an argument.
2.3 Explain causes of a local or global issue and the consequences on others.
2.4 Suggest and justify different actions to make a positive difference to a national or global issue.
3 Evaluation
3.1 Evaluate sources, considering the author and purpose, recognising that some sources may be biased.
3.2 Discuss the effectiveness of a source, making explicit reference to its development of an argument.
4 Reflection
4.1 Explain personal contribution to teamwork and identify targets for improvement.
4.2 Consider the benefits and challenges of teamwork experienced when working together to achieve a shared outcome.
4.3 Consider ways that personal perspective on an issue may have changed as a result of conducting research or exploring different perspectives.
4.4 Identify skills learned or improved during an activity and relate to personal strengths and areas for improvement.
6 Communication
6.1 Present information and arguments clearly with some reasoning, referencing sources where appropriate.
6.2 Listen to ideas and information and offer relevant and well-judged contributions that demonstrate understanding of the issue.
</td></tr>
</table>

Starting with collaboration skills: Lesson 1

Lesson 1 focuses on identifying what the term 'collaboration' means and exploring different team member characteristics.

CAMBRIDGE STAGE 7 COLLABORATION LEARNING OBJECTIVES

5.1 The team assign roles and divide tasks fairly, considering the skills of team members and time available, and work together to achieve a shared outcome

5.2 The team member introduces useful ideas to help achieve a shared outcome and works positively to resolve conflict, solve problems and encourage other team members to participate, when required

LEARNING GOALS

To start to:

- understand what the term 'collaboration' means
- identify some different team member characteristics

How will I know if I reach my goals?

Good for: Learners to give examples of their learning from the lesson. They can complete the table at any point in the lesson, but they might do it at the end.

Resources needed

Learner's Skills Book 7; Your own Language Support handout (if appropriate); Challenge topic (e.g. Water, food and agriculture); video clip(s) and debate questions (see Worked Example for the Main activity); equipment to show video clip(s); internet access; computers.

Prior learning (approx. 5 mins)

Good for: Building on previous knowledge, learning and understanding. This might be from Primary Global Perspectives, from other subject areas, or from previous Stage 7 Global Perspectives lessons.

Activity: Make a mind map of words/phrases relevant to the term 'collaboration'. Some might find this a challenge to start with but should be able to gain a better understanding after class discussion.

Differentiation: Learners work individually, share their ideas about what collaboration is in pairs and during class discussion.

Suggested answers/ideas: Answers will vary. Collaboration is working with others towards a shared outcome. Suggested words/phrases: work together; united; share; cooperate; discussion; with; jointly; participate; combine; partnership; alliance; group effort; teamwork.

Not topic specific.

Starter activity (approx. 10 mins)

Good for: Enabling learners to start identifying the type of characteristics needed for effective teamwork.

Activity: Learners decide which characteristics are important for a team to have when organising a charity event. They should try to explain why they think the team should have these characteristics.

Ways of working: Individual, with pair feedback.

Suggested answers: Answers/choices will vary. Any reasonable and relevant response. Encourage leaners to say why these characteristics are important/necessary or not. For example, after they have discussed with their partner, they might have changed their view and agree with their partner that sharing good ideas is the most important characteristic as, without these ideas, an event is unlikely to happen. Learners will probably identify **A**, **B**, **C**, **D**, **E**, **H** and I as important because they all help with effective teamwork. **F**, **G** and **J** are not helpful for effective teamwork.

Main activity (approx. 20–25 mins)

Good for: Enabling learners to work together in small groups to gain and share information and develop collaboration skills.

Activity: Show video clip (s) and ask learners to answer the questions individually. You can show a couple of short clips (see Worked Example).

For task 3, give each team a different question (see Worked Example for ideas). Teams discuss the questions together to complete the K, W, H parts of the table and will do research in Lesson 2 to complete the L (what we've learned) part of the table. Encourage learners to be specific (e.g. website addresses for the 'how' part rather than just writing 'internet') and to write three bullet points for each section of the table.

Differentiation: Group work as support – mixed-ability groups. Choice of video clip (see Worked Example). Refer learners to the tips about facts, opinions, predictions and bias.

Ways of working: Individually and then in small groups/teams.

Different opinions/perspectives: Encourage learners to consider the different opinions/viewpoints/perspectives explored in the video clip(s), as well as forming their own opinion about what they see/hear.

Learner response and feedback: Encourage learners to focus on the issue/ key points (facts, opinions, predictions, bias) in the clip(s).

Suggested answers/ideas: See Worked Example.

Worked Example for the Main activity

Challenge topic: Water, food and agriculture

Suggested video clips:

- Songs from Global Citizen about food waste: https://www.facebook.com/GLBLCTZN/videos/1317889278306837
- 'World is in our Hands' – food waste song: https://www.youtube.com/watch?v=38BxW3WdnRs

Question ideas for team discussion in task 3:

- Should governments forbid throwing away unused food?
- Is food waste a global issue?
- Can an individual do anything about food waste?
- Should customers in restaurants pay more if they leave food?
- Is food waste a national issue?

Suggested answers/ideas:

Issues: Food waste – personal (at home), restaurants, companies, and so on; world food hunger.

Examples from 'The World is in our Hands' song

- Fact: between 2010 and 2012, 807 million people suffered from being malnourished.
- Opinion: waste is a global pandemic.
- Prediction: by 2035, we will need to produce 70% more.
- Bias: how much our country wastes; make it change, I've finished my plate.

Websites for further information about food waste:

- https://friendsoftheearth.uk/food-waste
- https://www.youtube.com/watch?v=IoCVrkcaH6Q
- https://www.bbc.co.uk/bbcthree/clip/608f64a9-2b4e-4453-9be4-974e39fe845f

Independent reflection activity (approx. 5–10 mins)

Good for: Learners to give examples of how they might have participated in teamwork, for example, by contributing facts, opinions, predictions or examples of bias to the discussion about the text or by participating in discussion about the question given and completing the KWH part of their KWHL chart. Encourage learners to reflect on other skills as well as collaboration skills (research, analysis, evaluation, reflection, communication) they have used this lesson. This activity can be done in class, at home or in self-study time.

Starting with collaboration skills: Lesson 2

Lesson 2 focuses on using information gained in learners' KWHL charts to present an argument and reflect on the strengths team members brought to the teamwork.

CAMBRIDGE STAGE 7 COLLABORATION LEARNING OBJECTIVES

5.1 The team assign roles and divide tasks fairly, considering the skills of team members and time available, and work together to achieve a shared outcome

5.2 The team member introduces useful ideas to help achieve a shared outcome and works positively to resolve conflict, solve problems and encourage other team members to participate, when required

LEARNING GOALS

To start to:

- understand what 'collaboration' is
- identify skills of team members
- share ideas with team members

How will I know if I reach my goals?

Good for: Learners to give examples of their learning from the lesson. They can complete the table at any point in the lesson, but they might do it at the end.

Resources needed

Learner's Skills Book 7; Your own Language Support handout (if appropriate); Questions to research (see Worked Example for the Starter activity); internet access; computers.

Prior learning (approx. 5–10 mins)

Good for: Building on previous knowledge, learning and understanding. This might be from Primary Global Perspectives, from other subject areas and from Lesson 1.

Activity: Learners identify the skills that different members of their team possess.

Differentiation: Learners work in teams.

Suggested answers/ideas: Any reasonable and relevant response. Different teams will have different strengths/characteristics. The aim of the activity is to get learners thinking about the skills their team has.

Starter activity (approx. 5–10 mins)

Good for: Reviewing words/phrases relevant to the topic area/question given during Lesson 1 or a new question related to the topic that learners prepare an argument for in teams in the Main activity.

Activity: Show learners a set of questions to brainstorm relevant words/phrases for use in the Main activity. It's a good idea to use the same question from task 3 in Lesson 1 so that learners can complete the L part of their KWHL chart after research.'

Suggested answers: Any reasonable and relevant response, depending on the question (see Worked Example for questions).

Worked Example for the Starter activity

Challenge topic: Water, food and agriculture

Question ideas for teams:

- Should governments forbid throwing away unused food?
- Should there be laws against food waste?
- Is food waste a global issue?
- Can an individual do anything about food waste?
- Can a community do anything about food waste?
- Should customers in restaurants pay more if they leave food?
- Is food waste a national issue?

Main activity (approx. 20–25 mins)

Good for: Getting teams to work together to come up with arguments from a certain perspective for a research question and produce a presentation.

Activity: Teams need to decide which perspective they are presenting and relate their arguments to this perspective. Learners can do research and discuss their arguments and choose up to five arguments/points. They should find some evidence to support each argument ready for when they create their presentation. Encourage learners to go back to their KWHL chart in Lesson 1 to complete the L section with what they have learned from their research.

Differentiation: Team members support each other.

Ways of working: In teams.

Different opinions/perspectives: Encourage learners to value all the viewpoints/opinions/perspectives explored.

Learner response and feedback: Learners help each other prepare arguments for the perspective chosen.

Suggested answers: These will vary according to the question and perspective chosen (see Worked Example).

Worked Example for the Main activity

Challenge topic: Water, food and agriculture

Question ideas for teams:

- Should governments forbid throwing away unused food?
- Should there be laws against food waste?
- Is food waste a global issue?
- Can an individual do anything about food waste?
- Can a community do anything about food waste?
- Should customers in restaurants pay more if they leave food?
- Is food waste a national issue?

All these questions can be explored from the yes/no perspective to allow learners to produce arguments for each.

Suggested answers:

Our question: Should there be laws against food waste?	
Our perspective: Yes, there should be laws against food waste	
Arguments	
1	In France, supermarkets must give their unsold food to charities and food banks instead of destroying it. Source: https://www.theguardian.com/world/2016/feb/04/french-law-forbids-food-waste-by-supermarkets
2	People are starving. The United Nations Food and Agriculture Organization (FAO) estimates that approximately 815 million people of the 7.6 billion people in the world, or 10.7%, were undernourished in 2016. Source: https://www.worldhunger.org/world-hunger-and-poverty-facts-and-statistics
3	Supermarkets and restaurants should think twice about portion sizes as portion size is one of the issues people discuss when asked about why they waste food when eating out. Source: http://www.wrap.org.uk/content/portioning-and-plate-waste
4	It's estimated that about 1.3 billion tons of edible food items go to waste every year. Source: https://en.reset.org/knowledge/global-food-waste-and-its-environmental-impact-09122018
5	People will become less lazy and not buy food like fruits and vegetables 'just in case' and then end up throwing them away. Source: http://www.fao.org/save-food/resources/keyfindings/en

Independent reflection activity (approx. 5–10 mins)

Good for: Encouraging learners to consider the strengths they brought to the team and areas they need to improve on to be an effective team member. This activity can be done in class, at home or in self-study time.

Starting with collaboration skills: Lesson 3

Lesson 3 focuses on presenting the arguments from Lesson 2 and reflecting on the skills of team members.

CAMBRIDGE STAGE 7 COLLABORATION LEARNING OBJECTIVES

5.1 The team assign roles and divide tasks fairly, considering the skills of team members and time available, and work together to achieve a shared outcome

5.2 The team member introduces useful ideas to help achieve a shared outcome and works positively to resolve conflict, solve problems and encourage other team members to participate, when required

LEARNING GOALS

To start to:

- understand what 'collaboration' is
- identify skills of team members
- work in a team to produce a shared outcome

How will I know if I reach my goals?

Good for: Learners to give examples of their learning from the lesson. They can complete the table at any point in the lesson, but they might do it at the end.

Resources needed

Learner's Skills Book 7; Challenge topic and presentation notes from Lesson 2 (see Worked Example for the Main activity below); Your own Language Support handout (if appropriate); space for teams to present to each other; equipment for presentations, e.g. computers.

Prior learning (approx. 5–10 mins)

Good for: Building on previous knowledge, learning and understanding. This might be from Primary Global Perspectives, from other subject areas, or from previous Stage 7 Global Perspectives lessons (e.g. Lesson 2).

Activity: Learners put the criteria for presenting an argument in a presentation in order from most to least important. They can use this as a checklist for their own presentation in the Starter activity.

Differentiation: Learners work in pairs/teams. Discuss responses in class.

Suggested answers/ideas: Any reasonable and relevant response. There may be some disagreement, which is fine, and some of the criteria might be equally as important as others. The main thing is the discussion and the thinking that the activity generates.

Not topic specific.

Starter activity (approx. 10 mins)

Good for: Reviewing the presentation of arguments from Lesson 2.

Activity: Learners review their presentation, making any changes according to the criteria rating from the Prior learning activity. They could also use the questions in the Main activity as a checklist.

Differentiation: Learners are working in teams.

Suggested answers: Will vary.

Main activity (approx. 20–25 mins)

Good for: Judging the quality of another team's presentation and arguments.

Activity: One team presents to another team, and each team completes the table to give feedback (see Worked Example).

Differentiation: Learners work in teams to discuss and give feedback to another team's presentation.

Ways of working: In teams.

Different opinions/perspectives: Stress that the feedback given is the opinion of the team. There is space in the table for the evaluating team to give peer feedback and for the presenting team to record teacher feedback, self-assessment and targets for development.

Learner response and feedback: Learners ask each other questions as they are working as a team according to the checklist in the Learner's Skills Book 7: 'Did you think there was a range of visuals (text, images)?', and so on.

Suggested answers: Will vary according to presentations and feedback (see Worked Example).

Worked Example for the Main activity

Team: Karin's team		
Question: Should there be laws against food waste?		
Perspective: Yes, there should be laws against food waste.		
	Opinion	Comment
Were there a range of visuals (text, images)?		Well-chosen visuals
Was the type of font and size suitable for the audience?		Yes, easy to read
Was there a clear structure (beginning, middle and end)?		Conclusion not there
Was the content relevant?		Yes, very
Did the content answer the question?		Not really, as there was no conclusion
Were the arguments supported with evidence?		Some evidence but not all points had evidence
Did the presenters make eye contact with the audience?		Yes
Did they speak clearly?		Yes
Were all members of the team actively involved?		Karin did more than the others, and Allan did very little
Peer feedback comments: **Highlight(s):** Engaging presentation with lots of ideas relevant to the topic. **Area(s) for development:** Needs a conclusion to answer the question.		
Teacher feedback comments: Agree with peer feedback		
Self-assessment comments: Agree with peer feedback		
Targets for development: 1 Add a conclusion 2 Answer the question		

Independent reflection activity Self-assessment; Challenge topic review (approx. 15 –20 mins)

Good for: Encouraging learners to think about the skills used this lesson. Encourage learners to give an example in support of the skill used, for example, 'communication' and 'spoke clearly and slow enough for the audience to follow'.

Learners also complete the self-assessment to set their own learning targets before they move on. Learners think about and shade where they think they are at this time in their learning. 'With help' refers to guidance given (pointing a learner in the right direction, although examples should still come from the learner), for example, from you, other learners, previous work done by the learner in the Learner's Skills Book 7. For the Challenge topic review, learners explore the topic used in this section to develop collaboration skills. These activities can be done in class, at home or in self-study time.

Suggested examples:

5.1 *The team assign roles and divide tasks fairly, considering the skills of team members and time available, and work together to achieve a shared outcome.* Example: 'Collaboration is working together to achieve a shared outcome like a presentation. I am good at listening to others. This helped when I made my presentation page as I knew to add my evidence to my argument.'

5.2 *The team member introduces useful ideas to help achieve a shared outcome and works positively to resolve conflict, solve problems and encourage other team members to participate, when required.* Example: 'Including the images was my idea, and most of them were included in our final presentation to add further evidence to our argument. There was a disagreement about how much edible food goes to waste each year as we found different information, so we decided to use the source we thought was better, which was the United Nations source.'

Developing collaboration skills: Lesson 4

Lesson 4 focuses on asking questions to find out local information.

CAMBRIDGE STAGE 7 COLLABORATION LEARNING OBJECTIVES

5.1 The team assign roles and divide tasks fairly, considering the skills of team members and time available, and work together to achieve a shared outcome

5.2 The team member introduces useful ideas to help achieve a shared outcome and works positively to resolve conflict, solve problems and encourage other team members to participate, when required

LEARNING GOALS

To develop knowledge and understanding about:

- resolving conflict during teamwork
- working together towards a common goal

How will I know if I reach my goals?

Good for: Learners to give examples of their learning from the lesson. They can complete the table at any point in the lesson, but they might do it at the end.

Resources needed

Learner's Skills Book 7; Your own Language Support handout (if appropriate); Challenge topic and series of questions e.g. Water, food and agriculture (see Worked Example for the Starter activity); scenario for learners to produce questions (see Worked Example for the Main activity); internet access; computers.

Prior learning (approx. 5–10 mins)

Good for: Building on previous knowledge, learning and understanding. This might be from Primary Global Perspectives, from other subject areas, or from previous Stage 7 Global Perspectives lessons (e.g. Lesson 3).

Activity: Learners consider their learning from last lesson and can discuss with their partners and/or team.

Differentiation: Learners can look back in their Learner's Skills Book 7 at their Reflection, self-assessment and development targets from Lesson 3. Learners can work in pairs for support.

Suggested answers/ideas: Any reasonable and relevant response. Encourage honesty and that learners look back through the lesson to see if they are succeeding with their development targets.

Not topic specific.

Starter activity (approx. 10 mins)

Good for: Reviewing topic-specific vocabulary.

Activity: Give learners a list of four questions. Learners give ideas and thoughts to answer the questions to do with the topic.

Ways of working: Individual, in pairs and class discussion.

Suggested answers/ideas: Depends on the topic (see Worked Example).

Worked Example for the Starter activity

Challenge topic: Water, food and agriculture

Sub-topic: Food waste

Example questions:

1 What do you think the term 'food waste' means?

2 Who do you think is responsible for food waste in … (insert country)?

3 Why do you think so much food is wasted in … (insert country)?

4 What do you think can be done about food waste in … (insert country)?

Suggested answers:

1 Food waste / food loss is food that is thrown away or left uneaten. There are many causes of food waste during the producing, processing, retailing and consuming of it. Food waste happens at all stages of the food supply and value chain.

2 Answers will vary depending on country; for example, in Canada, consumers feel that they are most responsible for food waste. Others responsible for food waste include restaurants, supermarkets/grocers, government, farmers, food processors/manufacturers.

3 Answers will vary; for example, in Australia it is estimated that the total cost of food waste to the economy is about AUS $20 billion with 50% coming from households. The reason might be because people have lost their connection to food and where food comes from.

4 Answers will vary; for example, in the UK, you can buy and cook only what you need; don't throw away leftovers right away but make a creative meal with it for the next day; be more organised about food storage so you know what you have and when it needs to be eaten by; use food for garden fertiliser.

Main activity (approx. 20–25 mins)

Good for: Working in pairs and in teams to write questions to gain information about an issue/topic.

Activity: Learners work together to formulate questions for a specific purpose – see Worked Example. They complete the table with their questions. They can then discuss with another pair and produce the five best questions as a team. As a class, all the questions can be discussed, and the best five questions chosen. Remind learners of question starters (What? Where? Who? Why? How?).

Differentiation: Learners can work in pairs for support before sharing with their team. Some further research might be needed to come up with questions.

Ways of working: Individually, in pairs and in teams.

Different opinions/perspectives: Learners will be formulating questions to gain information to start to develop a local perspective about an issue.

Learner response and feedback: Encourage learners to help and support each other in teams. They can ask questions such as:

- What are you trying to find out?
- Do you think they will know the answer to that?
- Do you think there is an answer to that?
- Does that question help us find out … ?
- Is that question too difficult?
- Does that question require a fact/opinion as the answer?

Suggested answers/ideas: Depends on the topic scenario chosen. See Worked Example.

Worked Example for the Main activity

Challenge topic: Water, food and agriculture

Sub-topic: Food waste

Scenario: Interviewing kitchen staff at our school (might be a skype interview or could be face to face) about food waste to raise awareness via a no-food-waste campaign/pledge (to be developed in Lesson 5).

Interview questions:

- Why do you think students throw away food that could be eaten?
- Which foods are generally wasted?
- How much food is wasted per day / per week / per month / per term?
- What happens to the wasted food?
- Where does the wasted food go?
- What do you think are some ways that we can reduce the amount of food we waste in school?

Suggested answers: Answers will vary. Questions can be given to dinner staff to give enough time for learners to process the answers ready for Lesson 5.

Independent reflection activity (approx. 5–10 mins)

Good for: Encouraging learners to identify any conflict whilst working in teams to produce questions and to consider how this conflict was addressed. For example, not agreeing with an idea is a conflict and a way to resolve it is to say why you disagree using facts. This activity can be done in class, at home or in self-study time.

Developing collaboration skills: Lesson 5

Lesson 5 follows on from Lesson 4. Learners use information they have gained to create a shared outcome.

CAMBRIDGE STAGE 7 COLLABORATION LEARNING OBJECTIVES

5.1 The team assign roles and divide tasks fairly, considering the skills of team members and time available, and work together to achieve a shared outcome

5.2 The team member introduces useful ideas to help achieve a shared outcome and works positively to resolve conflict, solve problems and encourage other team members to participate, when required

LEARNING GOALS

To develop knowledge and understanding about:

- working as a team to produce a shared outcome
- contributing ideas to a shared outcome

How will I know if I reach my goals?

Good for: Learners to give examples of their learning from the lesson. They can complete the table at any point in the lesson, but they might do it at the end.

Resources needed

Learner's Skills Book 7; Your own Language Support handout (if appropriate); internet access; computers; resources to create shared outcome – paper/pens, and so on.

Prior learning (approx. 5–10 mins)

Good for: Building on previous knowledge, learning and understanding. This might be from Primary Global Perspectives, from other subject areas, or from previous Stage 7 Global Perspectives lessons.

Activity: Review learning about shared outcomes by learners giving as many examples as they can.

Differentiation: Learners can work in pairs and share with another pair (their team).

Suggested answers: Any reasonable and relevant response. Ideas: brochure; leaflet; presentation; charity awareness event; poem; song; story; pledge (see Worked Example for the Main activity); awareness campaign; video clip; podcast/audio recording, board game, and so on.

Starter activity (approx. 10 mins)

Good for: Reviewing information gained from last lesson in preparation for creating the team outcome.

Activity: Learners answer questions about the information they gained in the last lesson.

Ways of working: Individually, in pairs and whole-class discussion.

Suggested answers: Depends on topic and information gained.

Main activity (approx. 20–25 mins)

Good for: Creating a shared outcome to address a local issue.

Activity: Learners work in teams to create a first draft of their shared outcome (see Worked Example). They can share their first draft for feedback in the next lesson before finalising their outcome.

Differentiation: Learners work in teams to create a shared outcome. Different teams can produce different outcomes. Learners can refer to the answers to their questions in the Starter activity. Encourage them to share the workload; for example, one pair might need to do some further research whilst another starts to write sentences.

Ways of working: Teamwork.

Different opinions/perspectives: Learners are creating an outcome using information gained from a local perspective.

Learner response and feedback: Encourage learners to discuss their progress.

Suggested ideas: Teams can produce any outcome, but it should contribute to the issue they are investigating, e.g. to raise awareness about the issue; to promote …; to take action in support of … (see Worked Example below for an idea).

Worked Example for the Main activity

Challenge topic: Water, food and agriculture

Topic: Food waste
Shared outcome: No-food waste pledge/promise
Aim: To take action to help stop food waste

First draft of shared outcome

Almost 40% of all the edible food in our school goes to waste each term.

This term, we, ______________________________, pledge to do the following things to help reduce food waste. We will also encourage our families to help too.

1 ....

2 ....

3 ....

4 ....

5 ....

Here are some suggestions for actions you can take.

No-Food Waste

- Ask for smaller portions so you don't waste any food.
- Tell people what foods you don't like to avoid wasting them.
- Eat all the food on your plate.
- Try new types of vegetables to decide which ones you like and eat them.
- Make your own lunch so you will have things that you will eat.
- Keep a journal and record anything you don't eat and give reasons.
- Help mum/dad with the weekly menu and create a shopping list for these meals.
- Eat fruit and vegetables that are not perfect – a bit out of shape or bruised.
- Use any leftover food for compost in the garden/allotment or give to someone else for compost.
- Be more organised. Donate food to a food bank before it goes off if you know you won't eat it.
- Freeze any leftover food rather than throwing it away.
- Give any spare/leftover food to someone else; house maid; gardener; driver; neighbour; homeless person, and so on.

We are Champions at not wasting food.

We pledge to do at least five of these this term ☐
GOLD No-Food Waste Champions

We pledge to do at least three of these this term ☐
SILVER No-Food Waste Champions

We pledge to do at least one of these this term ☐
BRONZE No-Food Waste Champions

Signed: .... Date: ....

Independent reflection activity (approx. 5–10 mins)

Good for: Encouraging learners to reflect on their contributions to teamwork by asking them for their best idea and the skills they have used in the lesson.

This activity can be done in class, at home or in self-study time.

Developing collaboration skills: Lesson 6

Lesson 6 follows on from Lesson 5 and focuses on completing shared outcomes after feedback.

CAMBRIDGE STAGE 7 COLLABORATION LEARNING OBJECTIVES

5.1 The team assign roles and divide tasks fairly, considering the skills of team members and time available, and work together to achieve a shared outcome

5.2 The team member introduces useful ideas to help achieve a shared outcome and works positively to resolve conflict, solve problems and encourage other team members to participate, when required

LEARNING GOALS

To develop knowledge and understanding about:

- working as a team to produce a shared outcome
- contributing ideas to a shared outcome
- using feedback to improve a shared outcome

How will I know if I reach my goals?

Good for: Learners to give examples of their learning from the lesson. They can complete the table at any point in the lesson, but they might do it at the end.

Resources needed

Learner's Skills Book 7; Your own Language Support handout (if appropriate); internet access; computers; resources to create shared outcomes; example shared outcome document for feedback (see Worked Example for the Starter activity).

Prior learning (approx. 5–10 mins)

Good for: Building on previous knowledge, learning and understanding. This might be from Primary Global Perspectives, from other subject areas, or from previous Stage 7 Global Perspectives lessons.

Activity: Review learning about the importance of giving and receiving feedback.

Differentiation: Learners can work in pairs for support and share ideas with another pair.

Suggested answers/ideas: Any reasonable and relevant response. Feedback gives learners clear guidance on how to improve their learning. Feedback helps learners understand the skill being developed and the topic taught. It provides learners with the necessary information to improve their learning towards achieving learning objectives.

Starter activity (approx. 10–15 mins)

Good for: Developing understanding about how to give both positive and helpful feedback on each other's work.

Activity: Look at the example shared outcome document (see Worked Example) and decide on two highlights and one area for improvement. An authentic piece of learner work might be used. Ask learners to give and receive feedback on their draft shared outcome from Lesson 5 using the grid in the Worked Example below. Teams should then incorporate this feedback into the final version of their shared outcome.

Ways of working: Individually, in pairs and whole-class discussion.

Suggested answers/ideas: Depends on the work given (see Worked Example).

Worked Example for the Starter activity

Challenge topic: Water, food and agriculture

Example shared outcome document for feedback

<table>
<tr><td>Aim: To help prevent food waste locally</td></tr>
<tr><td></td></tr>
<tr><td>
Almost 40% of all the edible food

This term, We, ______________________, pledge to do the following things to help reduce food waste. Will also encourage our families to help.

1 ....
2 ....
3 ....

Some ideas ...

No-Food Waste
• Ask for smaller portions so we don't waste any food
• Eat all the food on the plate.
• Try new types of vegetables to decide which ones we like and eat them.
• Make our own lunch so we will have things that we will eat.

We are Champions at not wasting food.
We pledge to do at least five of these this term ☐
GOLD No-Food Waste Champion

We pledge to do at least three of these this term ☐
SILVER No-Food Waste Champion

We pledge to do at least one of these this term ☐
BRONZE No-Food Waste Champion

Names: ....
</td></tr>
</table>

Suggested answers: Highlights: Clear aim; outcome suitable for the aim; some good suggestions for preventing food waste; 'Champions at not wasting food' is a great label.

Areas for improvement: Need more suggestions to choose from; sentence starting 'Almost 40% … ' is not finished/clear; Need a word in front of 'Will'.

Discussion about feedback:

Stress to learners that feedback should be kind, specific and detailed, and helpful.

Kind	Specific & Detailed	Helpful
Use kind words and be positive	Give an exact idea of where and how the work can be improved	Give suggestions for improvements linked to the learning objective/ learning goal
Examples:		
You include topic-specific words and phrases well. There are some great suggestions, which I've highlighted. I love how you have added facts as evidence of the need to act.	In the first part, you could have included … Your evidence needs to support your idea. What about this fact instead? This idea is powerful because …	Perhaps next time, you could try … Have you looked at the Language Support handout to help with … ? Make sure you proofread to check you have included everything.

Main activity (approx. 20–25 mins)

Good for: Giving feedback and finishing shared outcome after feedback.

Activity: This leads on from the Starter activity where learners recap on the value of judging work and giving feedback. They share their outcome with another team and give feedback. Highlights can be in one colour and areas for improvement in another. It's always a good idea to encourage more highlights than areas of improvement. Ask learners to refer to the learning objectives/goals when judging the shared outcome.

Differentiation: Learners work in teams to give feedback and improve shared outcome.

Ways of working: In teams.

Different opinions/perspectives: Remind learners that giving feedback generally means that someone will be looking at the work from a different perspective, perhaps as the user of the outcome or the audience if watching/ listening to something.

Learner response and feedback: Learners are giving feedback to each other.

Suggested answers: Feedback will vary. See ideas for giving feedback in the Starter activity Worked Example.

Independent reflection activity; Self-assessment; Challenge topic review (approx. 15–20 mins)

Good for: Encouraging learners to consider what they used to think teamwork was and how their thinking might have developed.

Learners also complete the self-assessment to set their own learning targets before they move on. Learners think about and shade where they think they are at this time in their learning. 'With help' refers to guidance given (pointing a learner in the right direction, although examples should still come from the learner), for example, from you, other learners, previous work done by the learner in the Learner's Skills Book 7. For the Challenge topic review, learners explore the topic used in this section to develop collaboration skills. These activities can be done in class, at home or in self-study time.

Suggested examples:

5.1 *The team assign roles and divide tasks fairly, considering the skills of team members and time available, and work together to achieve a shared outcome.* Example: 'Collaboration is working together to achieve a shared outcome like a presentation. I am good at organising who does what. This helped when we completed our pledge as we managed to meet the deadline set.'

5.2 *The team member introduces useful ideas to help achieve a shared outcome and works positively to resolve conflict, solve problems and encourage other team members to participate, when required.* Example: 'Some of the suggestions were my idea, which meant that we used the information gained from the interview in our outcome. There was a bit of conflict as we were all talking at once, so I suggested we take it in turns. This helped when we made our outcome better after the feedback.'

Getting better at collaboration skills: Lesson 7

Lesson 7 focuses on reflecting on and evaluating teamwork.

CAMBRIDGE STAGE 7 COLLABORATION LEARNING OBJECTIVES

5.1 The team assign roles and divide tasks fairly, considering the skills of team members and time available, and work together to achieve a shared outcome

5.2 The team member introduces useful ideas to help achieve a shared outcome and works positively to resolve conflict, solve problems and encourage other team members to participate, when required

LEARNING GOALS

To get better at:

- reflecting on the effectiveness of teamwork
- reflecting on my own role during teamwork

How will I know if I reach my goals?

Good for: Learners to give examples of their learning from the lesson. They can complete the table at any point in the lesson, but they might do it at the end.

Resources needed

Learner's Skills Book 7; Your own Language Support handout (if appropriate); video clips for the Starter activity (see below); computer and internet access to show video clips.

Prior learning (approx. 5–10 mins)

Good for: Building on previous knowledge, learning and understanding. This might be from Primary Global Perspectives, from other subject areas, or from previous Stage 7 Global Perspectives lessons (e.g. Lessons 3–6).

Activity: Review all the skills used during teamwork. Encourage learners to give examples from lessons 3–6.

Differentiation: Allow thinking time. Learners list all the skills they have used during the teamwork. You can start them off – listening, writing (communication skills).

Suggested answers: Any reasonable and relevant examples.

- **Research:** asking/writing questions; looking for information; organising and recording information
- **Analysis:** exploring causes and consequences; gaining ideas from different perspectives; supporting shared outcome with evidence; completing shared outcome; identifying course of action
- **Evaluation:** judging which sources to use to provide relevant information; evaluating teamwork – strengths and limitations of the team and own work processes
- **Reflection:** reflecting on effectiveness of teamwork and own contribution to teamwork; identifying skills learned and how perspective on the issue changed/developed
- **Communication:** listening; reading; writing; speaking; producing shared outcome
- **Collaboration:** working in a team; taking turns; listening to others; sharing ideas, and so on.

Not topic specific.

Starter activity (approx. 10 mins)

Good for: Reviewing what good and bad teamwork looks like.

Activity: Show one or more of the video clips. Learners identify the key message(s) and other information from the video clip(s).

Suggested ideas:

Teamwork songs:

- https://www.youtube.com/watch?v=qQ99hq1vxgU
- https://www.youtube.com/watch?v=3WTeNpg_nVA

Example of good and bad teamwork:

- https://www.youtube.com/watch?v=fUXdrl9ch_Q

Motivational video clip about teamwork:

- https://www.youtube.com/watch?v=O-Hzzg1AtVs

The power of teamwork:

- https://www.youtube.com/watch?v=dJpIjC9hQtI

Key messages: Teamwork is important; you can achieve more as a team; teams are supportive and help each other; there's no 'I' in 'TEAM', and so on.

Not topic specific.

Main activity (approx. 20–25 mins)

Good for: Working in teams to reflect on their own teamwork during Lessons 3–6 and on the production of their shared outcome.

Activity: Discuss and complete the tables as a team.

Differentiation: Learners work in teams to review how they worked together as a team.

Ways of working: In teams.

Different opinions/perspectives: Encourage learners to be honest and give their own opinions.

Learner response and feedback: Encourage learners to ask each other questions such as:

- When did you participate?
- How often did you participate?
- What did you say?
- Which idea was yours?
- Did you keep the team on task? How?
- Did you help to resolve conflict? How?
- What feedback did you give to improve our shared outcome?
- Did you help to review our shared outcome? How?

Suggested answers: Answers will vary according to teams.

Independent reflection activity; Self-assessment; Challenge topic review (approx. 15–20 mins)

Good for: Encouraging learners to consider the skills they have improved this lesson and which ones still need improving, for example, joining in discussions, reflecting on work produced to evaluation it and give and receive feedback on its strengths and areas for improvement, and so on.

Learners also complete the self-assessment to set their own learning targets. Learners think about and shade where they think they are at this time in their learning. 'With help' refers to guidance given (pointing a learner in the right direction, although examples should still come from the learner), for example, from you, other learners, previous work done by the learner in the Learner's Skills Book 7. For the Challenge topic review, learners explore the topic used in this section to develop collaboration skills. These activities can be done in class, at home or in self-study time.

Suggested examples:

5.1 *The team assign roles and divide tasks fairly, considering skills of team members and time available, and work together to achieve a shared outcome.* Example: 'Collaboration is working together to achieve a shared outcome like a presentation. I am good at organising who does what and I noticed how good Maria was at dividing the tasks so that everyone was involved.'

5.2 *The team member introduces useful ideas to help achieve a shared outcome and works positively to resolve conflict, solve problems and encourage other team members to participate, when required.* Example: 'Some of the suggestions on our pledge were my idea. Other suggestions came from Jake. I encouraged him to share his ideas as we had discussed them but he hadn't shared them with the whole team.'

> Section 6 Communication

Introduction

The learning objectives and learning goals for communication skills for Stage 7 focus on the following:

- Communicating information
- Listening and responding

However, you might also find opportunities within these lessons to develop some of the other Global Perspectives skills. For example, when identifying ideas and evidence from different perspectives within different sources, and recording these ideas in their own words, not only will learners be developing communication skills, it is likely that they will also be developing their analysis skills.

The ideas given in this Teacher's Book 7 are suggestions only, and the activities can be used with any of the Global Perspectives topics for Stages 7 to 9, although Worked Examples are provided for some learning activities. It is hoped that the ideas in this Teacher's Book 7 will help you structure your lessons in an active learning way with input from you as the teacher to help guide and support learners to become more better at communicating their ideas and arguments.

Communication skills overview

Learning objectives	6.1 Present information and arguments clearly with some reasoning, referencing sources where appropriate 6.2 Listen to ideas and information and offer relevant and well-judged contributions that demonstrate understanding of the issue
Challenge topic ideas	Water, food and agriculture; Sustainability; Tradition, culture and identity; Changing communities
Key points	• Understanding what 'structure' is • Knowing that communication is about being able to present ideas in own words, and not simply copying and pasting someone else's ideas • Understanding the need to give credit to all sources of information referred to in the text by using a reference list • Knowing that there is a difference between listening and hearing • Understanding that listening is just as important as speaking • Realising the importance of feedback to develop communication skills

Language support	• Pre-teach key vocabulary: communication; argument; paragraph; structure; beginning; middle; end; introduction; conclusion; supporting evidence; logical; sum up; heading; reference; citation; critical; feedback; highlights; areas for improvement; transition words; active listening; passive; verbal and non-verbal feedback; paraphrasing. Also include any topic-specific vocabulary – Water, food and agriculture; Sustainability; Tradition, culture and identity; Changing communities.
Cross-skills links	1 **Research** 1.1 Construct relevant research questions. 1.2 Identify and begin to reference a range of print and multimedia sources and use them to locate relevant information and answer research questions. 1.3 Select an appropriate method and conduct research to test predictions and begin to answer a research question. 1.4 Select, organise and record relevant information from a range of sources and findings from research, using appropriate methods. 2 **Analysis** 2.1 Identify ideas and evidence from different perspectives within different sources on a given topic. 2.2 Explain how graphical or numerical data supports an argument. 2.3 Explain causes of a local or global issue and the consequences on others. 2.4 Suggest and justify different actions to make a positive difference to a national or global. 3 **Evaluation** 3.2 Discuss the effectiveness of a source, making explicit reference to its development of an argument. 4 **Reflection** 4.1 Explain personal contribution to teamwork and identify targets for improvement. 4.2 Consider the benefits and challenges of teamwork experienced when working together to achieve a shared outcome. 4.3 Consider ways that personal perspective on an issue may have changed as a result of conducting research or exploring different perspectives. 4.4 Identify skills learned or improved during an activity and relate to personal strengths and areas for improvement. 5 **Collaboration** 5.1 The team assign roles and divide tasks fairly, considering the skills of team members and time available, and work together to achieve a shared outcome. 5.2 The team member introduces useful ideas to help achieve a shared outcome and works positively to resolve conflict, solve problems and encourage other team members to participate, when required.

Starting with communication skills: Lesson 1

Lesson 1 focuses on identifying what the term 'communication' means and exploring how texts are structured.

CAMBRIDGE STAGE 7 COMMUNICATION LEARNING OBJECTIVES

6.1 Present information and arguments clearly with some reasoning, referencing sources where appropriate

6.2 Listen to ideas and information and offer relevant and well-judged contributions that demonstrate understanding of the issue

LEARNING GOALS

To start to:

- understand what the term 'communication' means
- identify some key elements of a text

How will I know if I reach my goals?

Good for: Learners to give examples of their learning from the lesson. They can complete the table at any point in the lesson, but they might do it at the end.

Resources needed

Learner's Skills Book 7; text(s) (see Worked Example for the Main activity); Your own Language Support handout (if appropriate); Challenge topic, e.g. Water, food and agriculture.

Prior learning (approx. 5–10 mins)

Good for: Building on previous knowledge, learning and understanding. This might be from Primary Global Perspectives, from other subject areas, or from previous Stage 7 Global Perspectives lessons.

Activity: Create a list of words/phrases associated with the term 'communication'. Learners reflect on the term 'communication'.

Differentiation: Learners work in groups, sharing their ideas. Put a time limit on. The idea is to get learners thinking about words to do with communication.

Suggested answers/ideas: **C**ontent; **O**pinion; **M**essage; **M**iddle; **U**nderstanding; Spoke**N**; **I**nformation; **C**onclusion; **A**rgument; **T**ext; T**I**tle; **O**rganisation; Writte**N**.

Answers will vary. Communication is a way of transferring information from one place to another, either by using spoken or written texts or by non-verbal means such as pictures and diagrams.

Not topic specific.

Starter activity (approx. 10 mins)

Good for: Enabling learners to start identifying the different elements in a text.

Activity: Learners decide which elements are important. They should try to explain why they think these elements are important.

Ways of working: In pairs and whole-class discussion.

Suggested answers: Answers/choices will vary. Any reasonable and relevant response. They are all important.

Main activity (approx. 20–25 mins)

Good for: Enabling learners to work together in small groups to explore the elements of a text.

Activity: Show learners a text (see Worked Example) and ask them to complete the questions in their Learner's Skills Book.

Differentiation: Group work as support – mixed-ability groups. Choice of text (see Worked Example). Refer learners to the tips about texts and text structure.

Ways of working: Small groups/teams.

Different opinions/perspectives: Encourage learners to consider the perspective that the ideas in the text come from, as well as forming their own opinion about what they read.

Learner response and feedback: Encourage learners to focus on answering the questions and giving examples.

Suggested answers/ideas: See Worked Example.

Worked Example for the Main activity

Challenge topic: Water, food and agriculture

Text idea:

IS THE WORLD RUNNING OUT OF WATER?

Water falls from the sky as rain, and we are surrounded by it with oceans that cover almost three-quarters of the Earth's surface. So, why are we so worried that we are running out of it?

As the population of the world increases, so does the world's need for clean, fresh water. Everything we do needs water. We need it for drinking, washing, growing food, and we need it for the construction and manufacturing industries. With more than 7.5 billion people living on the planet, and this number predicted to rise to 10 billion by 2050, the water situation is getting more critical.

The biggest concern is that most of the Earth's water resources are inaccessible, and those that are accessible are unevenly distributed across the planet. Currently, about one in every nine people living on our planet lacks access to clean, affordable water that they can reach within half an hour's walk of where they live. Water is hard to transport over long distances, and our needs are growing, both for food and industry.

It is estimated that almost 300 000 children under the age of five die of diseases linked to dirty water and poor sanitation every year. Others get sick and cannot go to school or work, missing out on education and opportunities to provide for their families.

Providing clean, fresh water to all those who need it is not only necessary for human safety, security and survival, but also has massive social and economic benefits as access to clean water lessens the burden on healthcare systems and enables those industries that need water to thrive, providing us with the resources we need to survive.

Reference

https://www.sustainabledevelopmentgoals/water

Suggested answers:

1 **a** Water is running out.

b Five paragraphs:

1. There should be an abundance of water but it's running out – links to the title
2. Population increases so increased need for water: drinking; washing; growing food; industry
3. Inaccessibility – hard to transport over long distances
4. Consequences of lack of clean water – sickness so time off school and work
5. Conclusion – sums up ideas – providing clean water is necessary for human survival and to lessen the burden on health systems and help industry thrive.

c Yes. Paragraph 3 about inaccessibility and supporting evidence that about one in every nine people does not having access to water within half an hour's walk of where they live follows on from paragraph 2 saying that the water situation is getting critical.

d Yes

e Yes

f Yes, and no – it's not accurate as it's just the website URL address

g Yes

Independent reflection activity (approx. 5–10 mins)

Good for: Learners to give examples of the best idea they heard, for example, that a paragraph is made up of an idea and then supporting evidence; a text is structured when it has a beginning, middle and end; a conclusion sums up points made in the rest of the text. Encourage learners to reflect on other skills as well as communication skills (research, analysis, evaluation, reflection, collaboration) they have used this lesson. This activity can be done in class, at home or in self-study time.

Starting with communication skills: Lesson 2

Lesson 2 focuses on using identifying key messages from listening texts and finding information to create an argument.

CAMBRIDGE STAGE 7 COMMUNICATION LEARNING OBJECTIVES

6.1 Present information and arguments clearly with some reasoning, referencing sources where appropriate

6.2 Listen to ideas and information and offer relevant and well-judged contributions that demonstrate understanding of the issue

LEARNING GOALS

To start to:

- understand what 'communication' is
- identify elements that make up a structured argument
- identify key ideas from texts

How will I know if I reach my goals?

Good for: Learners to give examples of their learning from the lesson. They can complete the table at any point in the lesson, but they might do it at the end.

Resources needed

Learner's Skills Book 7; Your own Language Support handout (if appropriate) Challenge topic, e.g. Water, food and agriculture; video clips (see Worked Example for the Starter activity), statements to research (see Worked Example for the Main activity); internet access; computers.

Prior learning (approx. 5–10 mins)

Good for: Building on previous knowledge, learning and understanding. This might be from Primary Global Perspectives, from other subject areas and from their last Global Perspectives lesson (i.e. Lesson 1).

Activity: Learners tick the elements they think make up a structured argument.

Differentiation: Learners can look back to the work done last lesson and refer to the tips in the Learner's Skills Book 7.

Suggested answers/ideas: They all contribute to a structured argument. A reference list is necessary for the supporting evidence. Perspectives are necessary, but the argument may be from only one perspective. The main outcome of the activity is that learners understand through discussion the elements and their importance in constructing an argument, which they will be doing in subsequent lessons.

Starter activity (approx. 5–10 mins)

Good for: Identifying key ideas/messages about the topic.

Activity: Learners watch the video clips and record the key ideas. They discuss with a partner before class discussion. See Worked Example.

Suggested answers: Any reasonable and relevant response, depending on the video clips (see Worked Example for suggestions).

Worked Example for the Starter activity

Challenge topic: Water, food and agriculture

Video clip ideas:

- https://www.youtube.com/watch?v=ZkStObhWjnIkey – Water crisis is a personal issue for women; they walk miles to fetch water for the family; new sanitation loan for a toilet; more time to raise their children and to work.
- https://www.youtube.com/watch?v=LSqan1xmMpY – Water crisis; 2.6 billion people lack clean water and a toilet; children miss school; mums walk miles; people get sick and die (over 4000 children); it's solvable.
- https://www.youtube.com/watch?v=FTNdElEypF8 – Water is in everything we do; makes drinks; for washing; growing salad; keeps us alive; world water day; be grateful for clean water.
- https://www.youtube.com/watch?v=JCJetUyl2pE – Make Sustainable Development Goal 6 the number one priority; help everyone to have fresh, clean water.

Main activity (approx. 20–25 mins)

Good for: Starting to write a structured argument in pairs.

Activity: Give each pair a statement (see Worked Example). If more than one pair has the same statement, they can give feedback on each other's work and share ideas at the end of the activity. Learners do research and complete the table with ideas for the beginning, middle and end of an argument about their statement. They should find some evidence to support each point they make in the middle section of their argument.

Differentiation: Pairs support each other.

Ways of working: In pairs, then in fours.

Different opinions/perspectives: Encourage learners to value all the viewpoints/opinions/perspectives explored and consider the perspective their argument is coming from.

Learner response and feedback: Learners help each other create their notes for the beginning, middle and end.

Suggested answers: These will vary according to the statement given (see Worked Example).

Worked Example for the Main activity

Challenge topic: Water, food and agriculture

Statement ideas:

- A sanitation loan is a good idea.
- There is a world water crisis.
- For many, water is accessible, but it is dirty.
- The water crisis is causing sickness and disease.
- There is enough water for everyone.
- Clean, fresh water is inaccessible for many.
- The water crisis is a personal issue for women.
- Water should be Sustainable Development Goal number one.

All these statements lend themselves to an argument with a beginning, middle and end.

Suggested answers:

Statement: There is a world water crisis.	
Beginning	There is a water crisis in the world today. This crisis is only going to get worse, and it affects women particularly. Everybody needs to recognise that there is an issue. Everybody needs to start doing something to help.
Middle	In Africa and Asia, the average distance people walk to collect water is about six kilometres. https://www.worldvision.org/clean-water-news-stories/walk-water-6k One child dies every two minutes from a water-related disease. https://water.org/our-impact/water-crisis Girls spend so much time collecting water they do not have time to go to school. https://www.un.org/sustainabledevelopment/blog/2016/08/at-start-of-world-water-week-unicef-highlights-how-girls-lose-time-collecting-water People can help by thinking about how much water they are using and wasting and by trying to save water where possible. https://friendsoftheearth.uk/natural-resources/13-best-ways-save-water-heatwave-or-no-heatwave
End	We have seen from … that there is a water crisis in the world today. Girls and women spend too much time collecting water in … and not enough time at school getting an education or at work. This crisis is only going to get worse unless we all do something about it such as … as suggested by …

Independent reflection activity (approx. 5–10 mins)

Good for: Encouraging learners to consider what they've learned in the lesson and how they've helped someone else to learn. Encourage learners to reflect on other skills as well as communication skills (research, analysis, evaluation, reflection, collaboration) they have used this lesson. This activity can be done in class, at home or in self-study time.

Starting with communication skills: Lesson 3

Lesson 3 focuses on creating the arguments from the notes made in Lesson 2.

CAMBRIDGE STAGE 7 COMMUNICATION LEARNING OBJECTIVES

6.1 Present information and arguments clearly with some reasoning, referencing sources where appropriate

6.2 Listen to ideas and information and offer relevant and well-judged contributions that demonstrate understanding of the issue

LEARNING GOALS

To start to:

- understand what 'communication' is
- state elements that make up a structured argument
- create an argument

How will I know if I reach my goals?

Good for: Learners to give examples of their learning from the lesson. They can complete the table at any point in the lesson, but they might do it at the end.

Resources needed

Learner's Skills Book 7; notes from the Main activity, Lesson 2; Your own Language Support handout (if appropriate), internet access and computers for further research if necessary.

Prior learning (approx. 5–10 mins)

Good for: Building on previous knowledge, learning and understanding. This might be from Primary Global Perspectives, from other subject areas, or from Lessons 1 and 2.

Activity: Learners write down three elements of an effective structured argument. After class discussion, they can add a further two elements.

Differentiation: Learners work in pairs. Discuss responses in class.

Suggested answers: Any reasonable and relevant response. Ideas covered in Lesson 2: conclusion; introduction; middle; supporting evidence; reference list; title/heading; punctuation; correct spelling; topic-specific words/phrases; paragraphs, and so on.

Not topic specific.

Starter activity (approx. 10 mins)

Good for: Reviewing notes made in Section 6 'Communication', Lesson 2: Main activity.

Activity: Learners review their notes and share with another pair who have the same statement to add to their notes. They will work with this pair to write their argument in the Main activity.

Differentiation: Learners work in pairs and in small groups/teams.

Suggested answers: Will vary according to the statement given.

Main activity (approx. 20–25 mins)

Good for: Working as a team to create an argument to read out aloud or record as a podcast.

Activity: Notes are used to write a final draft of the argument related to the statement given.

Differentiation: Learners work in teams to write the script. Each team member can be allocated a different part of the script, for example, one team member does the introduction; another the conclusion and the others the points in the middle. The team meets to share and amend their part before a final review once it's all put together. It can then be read out in class or recorded as a podcast for the next lesson.

Ways of working: In teams.

Different opinions/perspectives: Stress that the argument produced is the opinion/perspective of the team. Also encourage learners to look at different perspectives of the ideas they include in their argument, for example, the perspective of a non-governmental organisation might be different to that of a sponsored company or that given on a government website.

Learner response and feedback: Learners ask each other questions as they are working as a team according to the checklist in the Peer Feedback section.

Suggested answers: Will vary according to the statement and information gained by learners.

Independent reflection activity Self-assessment; Challenge topic review (approx. 15 –20 mins)

Good for: Encouraging learners to think about the skills they improved this lesson and those that still need improving. Encourage learners to give an example in support of the skill improved, for example, 'collaboration' and 'shared relevant ideas with team members'.

Learners also complete the self-assessment to set their own learning targets before they move on. Learners think about and shade where they think they are at this time in their learning. 'With help' refers to guidance given (pointing a learner in the right direction, although examples should still come from the learner), for example, from you, other learners, previous work done by the learner in the Learner's Skills Book 7. For the Challenge topic review, learners explore the topic used in this section to develop communication skills. These activities can be done in class, at home or in self-study time.

Suggested examples:

6.1 *Present information and arguments clearly with some reasoning, referencing sources where appropriate.* Example: 'Communication is a way of transferring information from one place to another, either by using spoken or written texts or by non-verbal means such as pictures and diagrams. I am good at knowing some of the elements of a structured argument, such as an introduction, a middle with points and supporting evidence, and a conclusion'.

6.2 *Listen to ideas and information and offer relevant and well-judged contributions that demonstrate understanding of the issue.* Example: 'I was able to give a piece of supporting evidence for the point about women being the most affected by lack of clean water supplies.'

Developing communication skills: Lesson 4

Lesson 4 focuses on listening to each other's arguments and giving feedback to improve the arguments.

CAMBRIDGE STAGE 7 COMMUNICATION LEARNING OBJECTIVES

6.1 Present information and arguments clearly with some reasoning, referencing sources where appropriate

6.2 Listen to ideas and information and offer relevant and well-judged contributions that demonstrate understanding of the issue

LEARNING GOALS

To develop knowledge and understanding about:

- what 'communication' means
- creating an argument
- presenting an argument

How will I know if I reach my goals?

Good for: Learners to give examples of their learning from the lesson. They can complete the table at any point in the lesson, but they might do it at the end.

Resources needed

Learner's Skills Book 7; Your own Language Support handout (if appropriate) Challenge topic, e.g. Water, food and agriculture; text (see Worked Example for the Starter activity).

Prior learning (approx. 5–10 mins)

Good for: Building on previous knowledge, learning and understanding. This might be from Primary Global Perspectives, from other subject areas, or from previous Stage 7 Global Perspectives lessons including Lesson 3.

Activity: Learners consider their learning from last lesson and can discuss with their partners and/or team.

Differentiation: Learners can look back at their reflection and their self-assessment and development targets from Lesson 3. Learners can work in pairs for support.

Suggested answers/ideas: Any reasonable and relevant response. An argument needs to include an introduction, a claim/statement about what someone thinks, reasoning and supporting evidence.

Not topic specific.

Starter activity (approx. 10 mins)

Good for: Reviewing topic-specific vocabulary.

Activity: Learners judge whether the text they are given (see Worked Example) is structured or not based on their knowledge and learning in this section. You can encourage them to look at the checklist in the Main activity (which they have already seen).

Ways of working: Individually, in pairs and whole-class discussion.

Suggested answers/ideas: Depends on the topic and text. See Worked Example.

Worked Example for the Starter activity

Challenge topic: Water, food and agriculture

Sub-topic: Water

THE WORLD IS NOT RUNNING OUT OF WATER

We are always hearing about how we are running out of water, and that fresh water is drying up globally. However, the fact is that there is, in theory, a limitless supply of water as we are surrounded by oceans. The real issue is not about how much water there is, and whether it's running out or not, it's about the cost of making the limitless supply of water we do have fit to drink.

We don't destroy water when we use it, we just make it dirty, and dirty water can be cleaned given the right equipment. Water can be and is being reused (EPA, 2018). Chances are that if you live by a river, some of your drinking water probably comes from a sewage treatment plant in a nearby town.

Cheap sources of water must be easily available, non-salty and generally clean to start with. These sources are not so easy to come by and mostly include rivers and lakes. The issue is that these sources of water are being used for agriculture to grow the food we need.

If we recycle dirty water and water that comes from the oceans, which is salty, then we will have an abundant amount of drinking water. However, clean, fresh water needs money to produce it, and countries and people living in those countries don't want to spend enormous amounts of money to produce fresh water. In addition, most people think that having access to clean drinking water is a basic human right, which means that they shouldn't be paying very much for it. Therefore, it needs to be cheap to produce.

To sum up, there is enough water in the world. Government agencies just need to be prepared to spend money on the equipment needed to clean dirty water without passing this cost onto consumers.

References:

Environmental Protection Agency (EPA) (2018). *Water Reuse and Recycling: Community and Environmental Benefits*. [Online] available at: https://www3.epa.gov/region9/water/recycling (Accessed 02/12/2019).

Suggested answers:

An example using the checklist from the Main activity below:

Statement:			
Is/are there ...			
	Yes	No	Notes
an introduction	✓		Links to the title and introduces the argument.
a conclusion	✓		Sums up the argument.
a middle with at least three points	✓		1 We can clean dirty water. 2 Water needs to be fairly clean to start with, but these sources are used for agriculture. 3 People think having clean water is a basic human right and therefore they shouldn't have to pay much for it.
supporting evidence for the points in the middle	✓	✓	For Point 1 only.
a reference list	✓	✓	Only one reference for point 1 (EPA), but it is accurate and gives not just the website address.
transition words/phrases	✓	✓	Some: to sum up; however; in addition.
accurate spelling	✓		
relevant words/phrases	✓		Recycle; dirty water; basic human right; sources of water; agriculture; grow food, etc.
punctuation	✓		
paragraphs	✓		Introduction, conclusion and three paragraphs for the middle.
a clear perspective	✓		There is enough water, but we need to pay to clean it.
a logical structure	✓		Points follow on from each other.

Stress that the text isn't perfect, but the checklist is a good way of reviewing their own work and the work of others. The learning is in the review of the text and the discussion, which will help learners create and improve their own structured arguments.

Main activity (approx. 20–25 mins)

Good for: Listening to and evaluating another team's argument.

Activity: Learners listen to each other's arguments – either read or played as a podcast. They complete the table with their observations and notes (notes can include/consist of the content of the argument depending on the statement chosen). They can then review the completed table and discuss with each other in order to give overall feedback on highlights (stars) and areas for improvement (wish).

Differentiation: Learners work in small groups, sharing ideas and feedback with each other.

Ways of working: In small groups.

Different opinions/perspectives: Learners are asked about whether the argument has a clear perspective. Encourage learners to state what this is.

Learner response and feedback: Encourage learners to help and support each other in teams. They can ask questions linked to the criteria in the checklist.

Suggested answers: Depends on the arguments presented.

Independent reflection activity (approx. 5–10 mins)

Good for: Encouraging learners to reflect on the effort they made in the lesson and to give at least one reason for their rating. Encourage learners to be in honest in their ratings for the effort they made in the lesson and to give at least one reason for their rating. This activity can be done in class, at home or in self-study time.

Developing communication skills: Lesson 5

Lesson 5 focuses on presenting information clearly and active listening to show understanding.

CAMBRIDGE STAGE 7 COMMUNICATION LEARNING OBJECTIVES

6.1 Present information and arguments clearly with some reasoning, referencing sources where appropriate

6.2 Listen to ideas and information and offer relevant and well-judged contributions that demonstrate understanding of the issue

LEARNING GOALS

To develop knowledge and understanding about:

- presenting information clearly
- listening actively to increase understanding

How will I know if I reach my goals?

Good for: Learners to give examples of their learning from the lesson. They can complete the table at any point in the lesson, but they might do it at the end.

Resources needed

Learner's Skills Book 7; Your own Language Support handout (if appropriate); internet access; computers; pictures (see Worked Example for the Starter activity); audio/video clips (see Worked Example for the Main activity).

Prior learning (approx. 5–10 mins)

Good for: Building on previous knowledge, learning and understanding. This might be from Primary Global Perspectives, from other subject areas, or from previous Stage 7 Global Perspectives lessons (especially Lesson 4).

Activity: Learners consider what is meant by the term 'active listening'.

Differentiation: Learners can work in pairs.

Suggested answers: Any reasonable and relevant response. Active listening is fully concentrating on what is being said rather than just passively hearing. It involves paraphrasing to show understanding and giving verbal and non-verbal feedback such as affirmations like 'I see', 'I know', and 'I understand', and nodding, leaning forward and making eye contact.

Starter activity (approx. 10 mins)

Good for: Presenting information clearly so that the partner understands what's in the picture/what the picture is about.

Activity: Learners describe the content of their picture (see Worked Example) to each other and try to either sketch the picture or to write down the details of the picture without seeing it, but by listening to their partner.

Ways of working: Individually and in pairs.

Suggested answers/ideas: Depends on topic and pictures given (see Worked Example for ideas). Class discussion about the importance of speaking clearly when presenting/describing, but also about actively listening to help understanding. Encourage learners to ask questions and use affirmations as well as non-verbal gestures to show active listening.

Worked Example for the Starter activity

Challenge topic: Water, food and agriculture

Ideas for pictures:

- A woman watering a cabbage field in Tanzania: http://www.ifpri.org/blog/agriculture-and-water-whom-much-given-much-will-be-required
- Residential recycled water filling station: https://www.cityofirvine.org/news-media/news-article/recycled-water-filling-station
- Water pollution: https://theberkey.com/blogs/water-filter/9-things-that-causes-water-pollution-and-its-possible-solution

- Watering plants: https://www.planetnatural.com/vegetable-garden-watering
- Find a picture from your area of a swimming pool or full bathtub.

Suggested answers/ideas: Learners can sketch or write the details of the picture as their partner describes it. You might ask learners to find their own picture about the topic/issue and then do this activity, but it will take longer.

Main activity (approx. 20–25 mins)

Good for: Developing listening skills and gaining key information.

Activity: Learners watch or listen to video/audio clips to identify the main message of each clip and any further information provided. (See Worked Example for ideas.)

Differentiation: Learners can discuss in pairs after each clip. A language support worksheet might be useful for some learners.

Ways of working: Individual, in pairs and whole-class discussion.

Different opinions/perspectives: Encourage learners to try to identify the perspective the ideas in the clips come from and record this in the 'other information' column.

Learner response and feedback: Encourage learners to discuss their ideas between clips.

Suggested answers/ideas: Depends on the clips (see Worked Example for ideas).

Worked Example for the Main activity

Challenge topic: Water, food and agriculture

Sub-topic: Water

Video clip ideas:

- Global water shortage: https://www.youtube.com/watch?v=aFFVRgL4ymk (first 3–4 mins)
- Solutions to providing enough water (desalination and reclaimed water): https://www.youtube.com/watch?v=-MiDqX7NYSY (first 3–4 mins)
- Water crisis affects everything: https://www.youtube.com/watch?v=BCHhwxvQqxg

	Main message	Other information
1	There is not enough water to go around due to increasing demand, population increase and the effects of climate change.	Water covers 71% of the planet. UN says that 2/3rds of the world's population will live in areas where there is a shortage of water by 2025. Impact of drought in Somalia is still felt – 0.25 million people died a few years ago because of a famine as there was no rain.
2	Desalination is something we can do. We can take salt out of water to provide enough water. Reusing water is another solution.	This is very expensive and very energy intensive. What do you do with the salt that's left over? This is a challenge. Reclaimed water can be used for golf courses, parks, swimming pools, etc.
3	Crisis because water shortage is only the start – it affects everything: education; health; poverty; women and children.	Nearly 1 billion people live without clean, drinking water globally. Because women and children collect water, they can't go to school or work.

Independent reflection activity (approx. 5–10 mins)

Good for: Encouraging learners to reflect on how they know they have been actively listening for gaining further knowledge and understanding about the topic. Encourage learners to reflect on other skills as well as communication skills (research, analysis, evaluation, reflection, collaboration) they have used this lesson. This activity can be done in class, at home or in self-study time.

Developing communication skills: Lesson 6

Lesson 6 focuses on listening to gain further information about the topic to produce a shared outcome in Lesson 7.

CAMBRIDGE STAGE 7 COMMUNICATION LEARNING OBJECTIVES

6.1 Present information and arguments clearly with some reasoning, referencing sources where appropriate

6.2 Listen to ideas and information and offer relevant and well-judged contributions that demonstrate understanding of the issue

LEARNING GOALS

To develop knowledge and understanding about:

- presenting information clearly and with some reasoning
- improving listening skills to gain information

How will I know if I reach my goals?

Good for: Learners to give examples of their learning from the lesson. They can complete the table at any point in the lesson, but they might do it at the end.

Resources needed

Learner's Skills Book 7; Your own Language Support handout (if appropriate) Challenge topic, e.g. Water, food and agriculture; internet access; computers; statements (see Worked Example for the Starter activity).

Prior learning (approx. 5–10 mins)

Good for: Building on previous knowledge, learning and understanding. This might be from Primary Global Perspectives, from other subject areas, or from previous Stage 7 Global Perspectives lessons (e.g. Lesson 5).

Activity: Review learning about active listening.

Differentiation: Learners can work in pairs for support and share ideas with another pair. They can review notes in their Learner's Skills Book 7.

Suggested answers: Any reasonable and relevant response.

We know if someone is actively listening by:

- affirmations – 'I see', 'Sure', 'Thank you', 'Agreed', 'Yes, indeed', and so on
- paraphrasing – repeating in own words
- asking questions to clarify understanding
- summarising what's been said
- non-verbal means – eye contact; nodding head; smiling; not fidgeting or looking away.

Starter activity (approx. 5–10 mins)

Good for: Developing active listening skills.

Activity: Read out each statement (see Worked Example) and ask learners to decide whether the statement is true or false. They will be able to check their answers in the Main activity. In this activity, they are ensuring that they understand the statement.

Ways of working: Individually.

Suggested answers/ideas: Depends on the statements given (see Worked Example).

Worked Example for the Starter activity

Challenge topic: Water, food and agriculture

Sub-topic: Water

Statement ideas:

1 Women in Africa carry about 20 kgs (40 pounds) of water on their heads.

2 One flush of a toilet in the developed world uses as much water as the average person in the developing

world uses for a whole day's washing, drinking and cooking.

3 People in the UK and America pay more for their water than people in developing countries.

4 95% of the world's population has a tap in their home.

5 In developing countries, it is the men and young boys who collect and carry the water.

6 Washing with soap and water can reduce disease by more than 40%.

7 Within 25 years, half the world's population might have trouble finding fresh water for drinking.

8 Diarrhoea kills 1.8 million children under the age of five each year because it cannot be treated.

9 On average people in the developing world use 400–500 litres of water every day. In the developed world people use on average 20 litres of water every day.

10 Carrying heavy loads of water over long distances will affect a woman's health.

Suggested answers:

1 True

2 True

3 False – in some countries like India, people pay more

4 False – only 30% of the world's population has access to piped water at home

5 False –girls and women collect and carry water

6 True

7 True

8 False – it can be treated

9 False – the opposite is true

10 True

Explain that learners will clarify their own responses with research in the Main activity.

Main activity (approx. 20–25 mins)

Good for: Researching to clarify understanding of an issue.

Activity: This leads on from the Starter activity. Learners work in pairs to find a source of information that supports their true/false response and, if the answer is false, learners correct it with a true statement. Pairs also create five new statements to share with another pair (they will need the answers) to say whether they are true/false.

Differentiation: Learners work in pairs to share ideas and then in fours to answer each other's extra five statements.

Ways of working: In pairs and then fours.

Different opinions/perspectives: Remind learners to check the type of website and which perspective the ideas come from, although they should be cross-referencing and checking and will write mostly factual statements.

Learner response and feedback: Learners can give each other feedback to check the quality of the statements:

- Is the statement relevant to the topic?
- Is the statement clear?
- Is there a definite true/false answer?
- If the answer is false, do we know the true answer?
- Do we have a mixture of true and false statements?

Suggested answers: Learners answers will vary (see Worked Example for the Starter activity for answers to the first ten questions).

Independent reflection activity; Self-assessment; Challenge topic review (approx. 15 –20 mins)

Good for: Encouraging learners to consider what they used to think about the topic and how their thinking might have developed/changed. This encourages personal perspective and how it's influenced by research and other perspectives.

Learners also complete the self-assessment to set their own learning targets before they move on. Learners think about and shade where they think they are at this time in their learning. 'With help' refers to guidance given (pointing a learner in the right direction, although examples should still come from the learner), for example, from you, other learners, previous work done by the learner in the Learner's Skills Book 7. For the Challenge topic review, learners explore the topic used in this section to develop communication skills. These activities can be done in class, at home or in self-study time.

Suggested examples:

6.1 *Present information and arguments clearly with some reasoning, referencing sources where appropriate.* Example: 'Communication is a way of transferring information from one place to another, either by using spoken or written texts or by non-verbal means such as pictures and diagrams. I am good at writing short sentences so that what I write is clear, e.g. 'In Africa, it is mostly women who fetch water.''

6.2 *Listen to ideas and information and offer relevant and well-judged contributions that demonstrate understanding of the issue.* Example: 'I was able to create two relevant statements for true/false answers.'

Getting better at communication skills: Lesson 7

Lesson 7 focuses on presenting information learned from research in Lesson 6.

CAMBRIDGE STAGE 7 COMMUNICATION LEARNING OBJECTIVES

6.1 Present information and arguments clearly with some reasoning, referencing sources where appropriate

6.2 Listen to ideas and information and offer relevant and well-judged contributions that demonstrate understanding of the issue

LEARNING GOALS

To get better at:

- presenting information with reasoning
- sharing ideas with others

How will I know if I reach my goals?

Good for: Learners to give examples of their learning from the lesson. They can complete the table at any point in the lesson, but they might do it at the end.

Resources needed

Learner's Skills Book 7; Your own Language Support handout (if appropriate) Challenge topic, e.g. Water, food and agriculture; picture (see Worked Example for the Starter activity); computers and internet access for further research if needed.

Prior learning (approx. 5–10 mins)

Good for: Building on previous knowledge, learning and understanding. This might be from Primary Global Perspectives, from other subject areas, or from previous Stage 7 Global Perspectives lessons (i.e. Lessons 1–6).

Activity: Review all the skills used during their Global Perspectives lessons. Encourage learners to give examples for the different skills.

Differentiation: Allow thinking time. Learners list all the skills they have used during Global Perspectives lessons. You can start them off – research, communication, listening, writing (communication skills). Set a time limit as there will be a lot.

Suggested answers: Any reasonable and relevant examples.

Research: Asking/writing questions; looking for information; organising and recording information.

Analysis: Exploring causes and consequences; gaining ideas from different perspectives; supporting shared outcome with evidence; completing shared outcome; identifying course of action.

Evaluation: Judging which sources to use to provide relevant information; evaluating strengths and limitations of the team and own work processes within teamwork.

Reflection: Reflecting on effectiveness of teamwork; own contribution to teamwork; identifying skills learned and how perspective on the issue changed/developed.

Communication: Listening; reading; writing; speaking; producing shared outcome.

Collaboration: Working in a team; taking turns; listening to others; sharing ideas, and so on.

Not topic specific.

Starter activity (approx. 10 mins)

Good for: Reviewing learning about the topic ready to make slogans / short and memorable phrases (in the Main activity) to get an important message across.

Activity: Show one (or more) pictures (see Worked Example for ideas) and ask learners to say what the picture is about. This can be done orally or written. Learners also think about what other information they want to know related to the picture. Encourage them to ask questions and come up with at least three questions. Questions can be discussed in class.

Suggested answers/ideas: See Worked Example.

Worked Example for the Starter activity

Challenge topic: Water, food and agriculture

Sub-topic: Water

Picture ideas:

1 African woman carrying water on her head: https://www.lds.org/media-library/images/woman-carrying-water-sierra-leone-689056?lang=eng&clang=ase

2 Children fetching water: https://www.worldvision.org/clean-water-news-stories/carrying-water-pain-neck

3 Running water tap: http://moneysavinghub.co.uk/index.php/money-saving-ideas/household/68-how-to-save-water-waste-and-slash-your-bills-at-the-same-time

Suggested answers:

- **Picture 1:** How far has she walked? How often does she fetch water? How much does she fetch? What is the water used for? Does she work too? Where are her children? Why does she fetch water / walk so far? Does she have to pay for the water? Is the water clean enough to drink / use for cooking?
- **Picture 2:** Are they all the same family? Do they go to school? How far do they walk? Is the water in the same town as they live? How often do they do this trip? Does mum/dad fetch water also? If so, how often and where from? Do they have to pay for the water?
- **Picture 3:** How much water is being wasted like this? How much water is wasted generally and how is it wasted? What happens to the wasted/flushed/run water? How much does it cost to waste water? What is this waste water used for? Is it used again?

Main activity (approx. 20–25 mins)

Good for: Working in pairs/small groups to create slogans based on the information learned about the topic. The aim is to make people aware of the situation, and perhaps suggest courses of action to help resolve the situation.

Activity: Discuss and complete the table as a team. They write a slogan, add a reason and where they got the information from to come up with their slogan. The aim is to make people aware of the situation and perhaps suggest courses of action to help resolve the situations in the pictures in the Starter activity.

Differentiation: Learners work in pairs/small groups to support and share ideas. Give Language Support handout if appropriate. Give example to start with (see Worked Example).

Ways of working: In pairs/small groups.

Different opinions/perspectives: Encourage learners to consider the perspective their slogan is coming from.

Learner response and feedback: Encourage learners to ask each other questions such as:

- What are we trying to say?
- Is the message relevant to the topic?
- Does the message make people aware of the issue?
- Do we give a reason why someone should do this?
- Is the message clear?
- Is the message short and to the point?

Also encourage groups to give feedback on other groups' ideas. The best slogans can be put onto paper/card and displayed around the school.

Suggested answers: Answers will vary according to groups (see Worked Example for ideas).

Worked Example for the Main activity

Challenge topic: Water, food and agriculture

Sub-topic: Water

Slogan ideas:

(NB these web addresses are just examples of web addresses for the table, and not meant to be accessed.)

Slogan	Reason	Information Source
1 Turn off the tap whilst brushing your teeth	Because you will save up to 760 litres of water per month	https://sustainability.ncsu.edu/blog/changeyourstate/6-times-you-should-turn-off-the-tap-to-save-water/
2 Persuade local councils to fix leaks	Because they will save up to 3 billion litres of water every day	https://utilityweek.co.uk/water-industry-loses-3-1-billion-litres-of-water-every-day/
3 Convince government to desalinate sea water	So more people have fresh drinking water / as a way of resolving the national water crisis	Water Desalination the Solution to the Water Crisis? https://www.youtube.com/watch?v=dfqcT-h7pX0

Independent reflection activity Self-assessment; Challenge topic review (approx. 15 –20 mins)

Good for: Encouraging learners to consider the skills they have improved this lesson and how they improved this skill, for example, this might be communicating – joining in discussions; analysis – giving a reason for their slogan/message; evaluation – giving feedback on another groups' work, and so on.

Learners also complete the self-assessment to set their own learning targets. Learners think about and shade where they think they are at this time in their learning. 'With help' refers to guidance given (pointing a learner in the right direction, although examples should still come from the learner), for example, from you, other learners, previous work done by the learner in the Learner's Skills Book 7. For the Challenge topic review, learners explore the topic used in this section to develop communication skills. These activities can be done in class, at home or in self-study time.

Suggested examples:

6.1 *Present information and arguments clearly with some reasoning, referencing sources where appropriate.* Example: 'Communication is a way of transferring information from one place to another, either by using spoken or written texts or by non-verbal means such as pictures and diagrams. I am good at writing key messages like "Turn off the tap when you're not using it."'

6.2 *Listen to ideas and information and offer relevant and well-judged contributions that demonstrate understanding of the issue.* Example: 'I was able to create two relevant slogans and give a reason for each.'